BACK PAIN SECRETS

Warning!

Back pain usually passes on its own, but if you have any of the following symptoms, you may have some severe problems:

* incontinence
* decreased feeling in your genital regions
* difficulty getting an erection
* weakness in your legs and feet
* back pain that wakes you up at night or becomes worse when you rest
* you've been in a major accident, like as a car crash
* the pain is unbearable

If so you should immediately get to a hospital!

This book is not a replacement for a doctor's examination. The longer you wait before you get treatment, the bigger your chances are of getting permanent damage.

BACK PAIN SECRETS

The Tactics, Routines, and Habits to Fix Sciatica & Back Pain Naturally without Drugs, Surgery, or Other Harmful Procedures

ROBIN WAKEHAM

What kind of book is this?

I've read hundreds of books, magazines and websites aimed towards back experts in preparation for this book. Many of them are completely unreadable to normal people. Still, they contain useful information on how you can recover from your back problems. That's why I've summarized the most important information so that you won't have to fight your way through Latin and other inessentials. When possible, I refer to official sources, but sometimes other writers express themselves better, and in these cases I have chosen to include them instead.

But, *Back Pain Secrets* is not meant to be a substitute for advice from doctors or other back experts. No books nor websites could ever replace real life meetings with skilled representatives in care, no matter the criticism I give them in this book.

This book includes referrals to patients, cases and colleagues that I have met during my years as a back expert. All the names and characteristics that could identify any person have been changed.

Back Pain Secrets

How to fix your lower back pain and sciatica leg pain naturally without drugs, surgery, or other harmful procedures...

2023 Robin Wakeham

This book is dedicated to Linda, my wonderful wife and our two children, Kelly and James. You are my family, my home and my strength in life.

Table of Contents

Part 1: First and foremost

Part 2: Back secrets

Part 3: The inconvenient truth

Part 4: A shortcut to efficient back treatment

Epilouge

Bibliography

Thank You

Index

PART 1:
FIRST AND FOREMOST

Six quick questions

This book is written so that you can find the right help quickly. Here are some short answers to the most commonly asked questions. You'll find more information further on in the book.

My back really hurts. What should I do?

Answer: I promise that I take you seriously. I believe you when you say that you are in pain, and I will give you all the information you need. Do this: Take a pain killer. Rest, but not more than a day or so. After that, it's better for you to keep moving. If it gets worse, contact your local health care services. In the UK you can reach the NHS helpline on 111 or on www.nhs.uk.

Who do I turn to with my back pain?

Answer: Your local general practitioner. If you are in the UK, you can find your closest GP practice on https://www.nhs.uk. You can also register with a GP practice by submitting a registration form with your health insurance number at the clinic.

Why can't I see the top dog (the orthopaedist) directly? Why do I have to see my GP first?

Answer: You're not the only person suffering from back pain. The GP will refer you to the right department – or fix your problem right away. Serious problems have priority. If your pain is radiating through your arms or legs – contact your GP right away so that you can get referred to a physiotherapist, x-ray or orthopaedist. Where your GP sends you depends on how severe your injury is.

Should I have surgery for my hernia?

Answer: If you want to. The possibilities and the risks of having surgery or not having surgery are approximately the same. An operation may be the only solution if you're experiencing severe problems. See more information on page 132.

Could alternative medicine help with my back pain?

Answer: Never use alternative medicine for severe issues. For smaller ailments, it could potentially work as a complement. If so, see a legit practitioner, otherwise your health insurance will not cover you. The person should have an education in the field from a larger institution, not just a weekend course.

Who decides which treatment I should get?

Answer: You do! No one can force you to undergo surgery or other treatments without your full consent. Make use of that!

Why are you still in pain?

YOU DON'T HAVE ANY MORE EXCUSES

You should be pain free!

You have probably read lots of other books or seen many back experts to get rid of your back pain. It leads us to the obvious question: Why are you still in pain then?

Yes, I'm asking *you*! Why are you still in pain after all of this? It could of course be due to a number of reasons, but after having worked as a back expert for approximately 15 years, I've seen one reoccurring cause time and time again with my patients. It's most likely the same cause that's behind your back pain too.

Instead of telling you right away, I'd like to tell you about a patient. This is how our first meetings went:

1. He came fifteen minutes late – got angry because I said it meant we had less time because of this.

2. He didn't bring any paperwork – including copies of medical records.

3. His phone rang and he picked it up. He spoke for a long time.

4. After the conversation he demanded that I start fixing his back immediately – no examinations were needed!

5. When I asked about his medical history, he brought up that he broke his pinkie finger when he was 6, and every ailment since.

6. Upon being asked what the problem was, he first claimed that the pain was in his lower back. Then further up too. And over his shoulder blades and between them, along his arms, down to his hands, a little in his fingers, over the front of his body and down his legs. In the end: "It hurts everywhere!"

7. He couldn't tell me how much it hurt – on a scale, he was

off the charts.

8. He had been to a multitude of back experts and they'd done "everything: massage, cracked my back, put needles in me, given me exercises. Nothing's helped!"

9. He wanted to extend the meeting to ask if the insurance company would give him any money.

10. He didn't have any cash and he'd forgotten his NHS number.

11. He got angry when I said that we weren't open outside business hours.

12. He cancelled his next appointment, the same day it was meant to take place.

13. He ignored, forgot or didn't bother with the exercises he was given.

14. He came back with a worse back pain since he had helped a relative with "some garden work". It turned out he'd carried heavy buckets and sat hunched up on the ground. He had also been on a short cruise and *danced* and headbanged all night in hard clogs.

15. He continued to complain about me not "fixing" his back and after three visits he stopped coming – probably to move on to the next back expert and start all over again.

If you think that I'm making fun of one poor patient that can't defend himself, I can tell you that this isn't any one patient. I also haven't combined several patients into one very bad one to show you all the potential mistakes patients do. Every single back expert has seen these kinds of patients, that check off at least 10 out of 15 of the characteristics above. Not once, but *a few times a month*! No wonder those patients are still in pain. Chances are, that's the same reason why you're still in pain.

In other words, most of what we've learned during six years of education (often even more!) is ignored by the majority of all patients. Often, patients follow the advice of evening papers instead and then they wonder why they aren't improving.

Imagine you're experiencing problems with your car. If the mechanic said that you need to change the entire suspension to not wreck the car – would you not do that? Would you come up with excuses next time about "forgetting" to have the suspension replaced? Why would you care for your body any less?

Do you really want to get rid of your pain?

Do you want to get rid of your back pain? Really? Don't answer until you've thought about it properly. Give yourself a few minutes to think about the question. First, think about what you have to gain when you're in pain? Isn't the sympathy and the household work you're escaping pretty sweet benefits. Do you really want to give this up?

You're the one in charge. I'm not going to baby you since it won't help you, and I won't try to convince you, since you'll be lacking the necessary motivation if I do. I can only prescribe the medication. You're the one who has to take it. So, will you? Is the pain so severe that you're motivated to do something about it? How far are you willing to go to get rid of the pain? Are you ready to leave your comfort zone or are you just reading this book for fun?

The reason I'm pushing you to say ”Enough is enough! I don't want to be in pain!" is because it's important that you're willing to *change your behaviour*. You won't get rid of your back pain by reading a book, nor even starting to exercise. Life changes and breaking habits are required. It may sound like a cliché, but I have patients every week who refuse to change their behaviour – and then they come back with back pain, again and again. I've met thousands of patients during my 15 years as a physiotherapist, and those who are prepared to change their lives have a bigger chance to make a full recovery.

The Swedish Agency for Health Technology Assessment and Assessment of Social Services write thorough reports on the best treatments every year. In 2010 they wrote a report about rehabilitation for long-term pain. The report emphasized specifically how important it is to change your behaviour for a long-lasting result.[1] So it's not just me and my book.

But how do you change your behaviour to avoid back pain? That's what this book is about.

In actual fact, I can promise that if you follow the advice in this book and do not improve within six months, I'll give you *your money back!*

---

1 You'll find the entire report on SBU's website: http://www.sbu.se/sv/Publicerat/Gul/Rehabiliteringvidlangvarigsmarta/

Inconvenient Back Pain Challenge Nr. 1

I n this book, there are 12 inconvenient back pain challenges. I've named them that because they challenge you to get rid of a certain behaviour.

Imagine that you have 12 large boulders in a backpack. They're the cause of your back pain. We're going to remove these one by one, so that your back can function better. If you skip one of the challenges, or don't do them properly, the boulders will stay in the backpack.

Do this to get rid of the first boulder:

You can easily save both time, energy and money, and also receive better treatment if you once and for all get your medical history in order. Get a folder and mark it with the title "Back Bible". Then, take time off of work and phone the GP, the orthopaedists, physiotherapists, chiropractors, naprapaths etc. that you have previously met with. Every single one! Ask them to send you a copy of your records and what they've done with your back and the results of the treatments. You're fully entitled to this according to the Data Protection Act. Don't forget to ask the GP or the x-ray department to send copies of possible x-rays, surgery records and similar things. Put all the papers in the folder in chronological order.

Don't come up with any excuses! Excuses is one of your problems. Decide to take full responsibility for your back. No one else will. That begins with your "Back Bible". Prove that you can handle the responsibility.

Why should you read this book?

YOU'LL BE SURPRISED

Everyone's confused, it's not just you

I'm guessing that you, just like many other patients are confused. What is the deal? There's so much information everywhere, no ordinary person can be sure of what's what. What's the difference between treatment 1 and 2? What should I do to recover quickly? What happens if I never make a full recovery?

The confusion is made worse since each practitioner seem to contradict one another. Many back experts advocate their own field above all others. Your friends are the same. One of them tell you that the chiropractor is the best option and another recommends yoga, while yet another claims that surgery saved his back. What should you choose? What's right for you?

One thing that we can agree on is: you can't do it all. You have to choose.

Everyone's just as confused as you are. That's why all the evening papers and health magazines try to get you to buy into the latest methods. That's also why it's important that you resist. Don't buy into just anything. Stop trying all the methods *a little bit*. Your back will not get better by doing this[2].

Your best bet to get rid of your back pain is to talk to a back expert, so that you can agree on a plan of action together and that you then follow that accordingly.

In summary: don't try everything. Pick one thing and do it properly.

---

2 If anyone has made a full recovery with one of the latest trend methods, it's usually because the back pain has passed naturally, and would have no matter what actions the person took..

Who gets back pain?

Everyone should have healthy backs, and most people can, too. But back pain and problems with your neck is the second most common cause for people going on sick leave[3], and it's the most common cause for people going to the hospital. All ages suffer from this, both sexes, and all occupational fields and society classes. It's just as hard for everyone. Every year this costs the Swedish society around 2,5 billion pounds![4]

But in my daily work, I see two kinds of reoccurring patients all the time. Maybe you belong to one of these.

1. The stressed business man

This type is most often a man, and usually performance oriented. He works 70-80 hours a week, have everything under control and shoulders a huge responsibility. No rest for the weary. The family is a blur on the other side of the room. Adrenalin, coffee and kicks from work keep him awake. The anger is rarely far away, especially towards anything that keeps him away from work. That's the reason why he doesn't really want to come and see me. After all, there is a chance that he would be perceived as weak.

2. The self-sacrificing woman

The other kind is usually a woman. She's nervous and wants to please everyone. That's why she prioritizes everyone but herself. The advantage is that she is caring. The disadvantage is that she always has a bad conscience, feels powerless and thinks that she is an inconvenience to others. She wants a lot of things but doesn't know which end to start with.

Sure, other kinds of people also have back issues, but according to my experience it's not at all to the same extent. The common factor

3 The most common cause is having a cold.

4 "Ont i ryggen, ont i nacken", http://www.sbu.se/sv/Publicerat/Gul/Ontiryggenontinacken/. The Swedish Agency for Health Technology Assessment and Assessment of Social Services, 2000. There is no more recent information available.

for most back patients is, as I'm sure you've already figured out, high stress levels.

This means that if you are experiencing back pain, you don't want to read a book that brings up the same old exercises, preaches how to live correctly or promises a lot and delivers nothing. You don't want repetition. You want straight answers, so that you can recover quickly.

That's why it's worth emphasizing: the fastest way to recovery is *not* to start immediately or rush. It may sound like a paradox, but maybe if I put it like this you'll understand what I mean:

> *"We cannot solve our problems with the same thinking we used when we created them.*
>
> *– Albert Einstein (1879-1955),*
> *German-Swiss-Austrian-American physicist*

Up to this point you've stressed and used a certain strategy to recover. It's clearly not worked. To increase your chances of recovery[5], you need to relearn some things. You need new tools. You need to see the world a little differently.

Most of all, you need to get used to being without things that make it more difficult for you to recover.

5 No one can guarantee a full recovery, but you can increase your chances.

I'm a back expert with back pain

> *"Any intelligent fool can make things bigger, more complex, and more violent. It takes a touch of genius – and a lot of courage to move in the opposite direction.*
>
> *Ernst F. Schumacher (1911-1977), British economist*

I have back pain. There are many reasons for this, but a clash with a two-meter guy in full hockey equipment isn't the best starting point if you want a solid back.

Since then, I've had to exercise and go through surgery, but in spite of that, I'm not fully recovered. The operation was absolutely necessary for me to be able to think, and had I not exercised, my back pain would have gotten worse.

But there was a time when neither one of those things were my biggest issue.

I finished my master's degree in 2005 while at the same time working as a physiotherapist. Those were only my day jobs. At night, I was building an e-commerce site. My business idea was to sell quality products for everyone suffering from back pain. The Tempur mattresses became my best sellers and money started to roll in. Since I didn't think three full-time jobs were enough, me and my wife also had our first child around this time. I didn't sleep more than 3-4 hours each night.

Soon, I'd developed a taste for e-commerce and started another two international web shops. Somewhere along the way I lost track of day and night, but I was so high on adrenalin and coffee that the World Anti-Doping Agency would have disqualified me if I'd had a urine test done. For some reason, I was having a reoccurring back pain more often than usual.

It wasn't long before... I discovered an exercise tool on TV-shop that actually worked to train your back. The decathlete Henrik Dagård was the front figure in Sweden for the *Aerobix Shaper*, "the world's smallest gym". In the end, the inventor of this exercise tool gave me and my American partner Robert the rights to market this tool in the US. We recorded advertisements and negotiated with TV channels and so on. At this point my life puzzle consisted of 10,000 pieces, so I tried to become more efficient and read everything I could find on *time management*. This lead to me having time for even more things, and I was running around between my projects like an Energizer Bunny. My back hurt even more, and I couldn't understand why since I was doing all the things I told my patients to do.

My readjustment

My turning point came in 2008. I started to resent the life I was living more and more. All the projects, my physio therapy practice and the e-commerce sites did bring in some money, but I was working 12 hours a day, every day of the week. I spent more time with my phone and laptop than with my wife and child. I couldn't keep it up.

During the summer we went on a holiday for a week. I didn't enjoy a single moment of it, I mainly sat in internet cafés cussing, miserable over the fact that I'd lost control over my normal life. When the week was up, I gradually realized we hadn't followed through on almost any of the plans we'd made for the holidays: no long breakfasts and no romantic walks along the beach. So, we decided to extend the holiday, since I needed more time.

The first day of the extra two weeks, I had a nervous breakdown. I was forced to slow down. It meant that I managed to recover for the first time in many years. We even found time for a few long breakfasts and a couple romantic walks. My back got better, even though I skipped all my exercise.

Once I was back at work, I decided to not continue at the pace I had been going at. I sat down and started to identify the important things in my life. My family was very high up on the list, and all the small projects I spent time on weren't even part of the foot notes.

That's when I turned to a very successful entrepreneur friend. "The Tiger", as I called him, is always cool and still fast as lightning. When I told him that I was losing my marbles, he just smiled.

"I think you're ready for the 80/20 Principle." he said. "I was introduced to it several years ago in New York, I was in the same situation then that you are now." Then he looked at me seriously and said: "You should be happy that you've hit rock bottom." "Happy?" I questioned. "It's because you're feeling this shitty that you're forced to change your life to survive and not just scratch the surface."

The Tiger continued to explain the great impact the 80/20 Principle had had on him and a million other people, not just within the business world where it first became famous, but also as an efficient tool to manage stress and improve life quality. Then he went into more detail of what the 80/20 Principle was really about.

The 80/20 Principle

> *"The 80/20 Principle asserts that a minority of causes, inputs or effort usually lead to a majority of the results, outputs or rewards. Taken literally, this means that, for example, 80 per cent of what you achieve in your job comes from 20 per cent of the time spent. Thus, for all practical purposes, four-fifths of the effort – a dominant part of it – is largely irrelevant. This is contrary to what people normally expect."*
>
> *RICHARD KOCH (BORN 1950), AMERICAN ENTREPRENEUR AND AUTHOR, 80/20-PRINCIPLE, CHAPTER 1*

That time isn't enough for everything we want to do is so common that there's a huge market for teaching people how to fit in more in the same amount of time. But a lot of people forget that these aren't the things they really want to do. That's why they're stuck in different time management systems or walk around feeling unhappy about life.

The solution is based on two principles:

1. Identifying the important things in your life
2. Eliminating everything else[6]

6 This entire section is inspired by Timothy Ferriss' 4 hour work week, Richard

This means that you will live a simpler life, without many of the things that are taking up your time today. If you're completely honest – do you really have to check your emails more than twice a day? How much time do you spend watching TV? How often do you go to the shops without knowing exactly what you're going to buy or maybe even without money to shop for? Do you walk into the kitchen every now and then, just to check what's in the fridge because you're peckish? How many times do you look over the same bill before you pay it?

All of these things don't take up very much time individually but put them together and they take up to 80% of the time you are awake! This means that the things you actually get done happen during the remaining 20% of the time.

Think about it! By doing those 20 percent that actually produce results and skipping the remaining 80%, you'll have more time. In other words: by *doing less,* you can get more done.

Koch The 80/20 Principle, 1998, updated edition 2008 and Doubleday and Leo Babauta The Power of Less, Hyperion 2009.arbetsvecka, Richard Koch *The 80/20 principle*, 1998, uppdaterad upplaga 2008, Doubleday och Leo Babauta *The power of less*, Hyperion 2009.

Inconvenient Back Challenge Nr. 2

To remove the second boulder (you did do the first inconvenient back challenge, right?), do a 80/20 analysis. This means that you have to find the important things in your life. When I first did the 80/20 analysis, there were 10 things on my list, Now, I've removed everything but three things that create 80% of my happiness, there are:

* spend at least 2 hours with my wife and kids
* exercise daily, for at least 1 hour
* write daily, for at least 2 hours

It's important that you start with things that are important to you. It could be things you've always wanted to do, like your life goals. Without a doubt, they are things that you don't believe can be achieved or that other people think can't be achieved.

If you don't discover what these things are, you're probably going to continue to live with your bad habits – and it's your bad habits that are the cause of your back pain!

This book will teach you how to give up some of your bad habits, such as stress, complaining, spending time with friends who steal your energy, giving up exercise time again and again, being shy, eating too much and never finishing projects and lacking a purpose in life. These things affect your back.

But first, you have to identify what's important to you.

How you can find your way around this book

A common misconception when you're looking for treatment is that you hand yourself over to someone else. Unfortunately, you have to think for yourself when you're looking for treatment.

Because there are imbeciles in health care too, and there are plenty of people who know half of what they think they know. Not everything doctors and people working in health care say is true.

That's why this book is divided into four parts where you can learn to see the difference between truth and lies so that you can avoid back pain in the future:

PART 1. This is where you are now.

PART 2. Back Pain Secrets eliminate five of the most common and dangerous statements of how you can get rid of your back pain. Just seeing through these lies will ease your pain, but eventually you'll start to notice the pattern behind the lies and that will make it easier for you to find the right treatment, whether it's for your back or not. You will see that the power ratio will shift between you and the back experts.

PART 3. The inconvenient truth will take you behind the curtains of the back experts' practices and give you useful tools to find out the truth behind your back pain. Five tough truths will challenge you and take you outside your comfort zone so that you'll always receive the correct information. What I describe as truth isn't "my truth" but things that are backed up by both science and my colleagues' collected experiences. This is how you take back control of your medical story.

PART 4. The shortcut to the best back treatment is the most hands-on part, it includes lists and step-by-step guides for how you can find experts and help you didn't know existed, to prices you didn't know were possible and what questions to ask in the process. The idea is that you can use this part before, during and after your meetings with a back expert – and sometimes *instead* of seeing one. This part will give you everything you need to change things.

However, you should be aware that you will meet some resistance as you become more sceptical to what back experts are telling you. Some will attempt to get on top of you (not literally). Others will try to confuse you. As long as you know the difference between the lies and truths that I introduce in this book, you will stand a better chance of revealing them and find someone who genuinely have your best interest at heart. You deserve it!

PART 2: BACK SECRETS

"If you have no doubt, you are not sane.

– *Tage Danielsson (1928–1985), Swedish comedian.*

"Two politicians are having an argument. One of them stands up and says, "You're lying!" The other one answers, "Yes, I am, but hear me out.'"

– *Aaron Sorkin, American script writer, the TV program The West Wing, "What kind of day has it been", 2000*

Real experts vs. quacks

WHILE WAITING FOR THE RED FAKE MOUSTACHES

"It's just as well that there are lies – for what if everything we heard was true.

– Albert Engström (1869-1940), Swedish cartoonist and author

There are too many lies in health care to spend a great amount of time on the quacks in a book as short as this one – even though the quacks cause a lot of damage to many people. Luckily, other people have written good information in more detail about this.[7] Unfortunately, quacks don't wear oversized fake moustaches that are easily recognised. Without being an expert yourself, it can be very difficult to tell which back expert to listen to and trust. The placebo effect makes it especially difficult to know what makes an efficient treatment and what's all talk.

That's why I'm including a short summary of the differences between quacks (QK) and the real experts (RE):

QK value a single publication or person highly
RE value a great amount of unbiased science highly

QK stick to old theories
RE continuously test and re-evaluate old beliefs and new work that can be done to find better methods and products

QK have theories that demand a positive attitude
RE have theories that work even if you're unsure or negative

QK almost always require you to pay out of your own

7 For example Simon Singh & Edzard Ernst, Trick or Treatment?, 2008, Penn & Teller's TV show Bullshit!, and James Randi, Faith Healers, 1987.

pocket

RE are almost always cheaper because the treatment is supported by the country, municipality or the state

QK use the ”They helped me” advertisement to cover any failures

RE let knowledge speak for itself and bring up existing cases for an unbiased view

QK claim to be able to cure everything, or almost everything with one treatment

RE only treat ailments where the treatment has been proven effective

QK apologise if you’ve been mistreated, and (maybe) give you a discount on the treatment

RE are responsible under and controlled by the National Board of Health and Welfare

This may seem too simple. Sure, there are a lot of things that are right between these two stereotypes, but most treatments are closer to one of them, rather than in-between. Generally speaking, it’s good to visit a back expert that has studied more than a weekend course, preferably a few years at an established institute.

For more detailed information about the different treatments, see part 4.

The unreliable back experts

"All lies are deeply set in need. But need can vary."

– *Frithiof Brandt (1892-1968), Danish philosopher*

It's easy to think that only quacks lie about how you should look after your back and ease the pain. They lie so clearly, it's easy to see and prove that they're wrong. But that's not the case. Even back experts with proper education and who are often right could give you lesser advice than you're worth.

When real back experts lie, it's not only harder to prove, but it's also devastating. You should be able to trust them, since they've been approved by the National Board of Health and Welfare!

In this section, you'll encounter five lies that you're likely to hear when you see a back expert. These are big lies that could completely affect the future function of your back.

I can't say how many times I've encountered these lies from my colleagues, but it's at least several hundred times. All back experts are aware that they are spreading these lies. I've made myself guilty to the very same lies.

Yet, it's almost impossible to hold someone liable for these lies. They're too common, and too great to do anything about. Maybe.

But, I'm not comfortable with lying, I want to speak the truth, even if that makes my job more difficult. I want to tell the truth for your sake – so that you can make better decisions and because I believe it will speed up your recovery.

Inconvenient Back Challenge Nr. 3

Have you done the previous two challenges? If not, go back, so that you have a back bible and know what's important in your life.

Soon you'll find out what us back experts lie about. However, before that we have to remove yet another boulder. This boulder is about breaking habits. As Aristoteles said: "We are what we repeatedly do. Excellence is not an act, but a habit." If you're stressed and running around putting out fires in your work or in life, but never manage to get things under control – then it is a habit, not a matter of circumstances. The common denominators are you and your habits. All habits can be broken, if you want to. The only thing that is required is the word "no". The word "no" is equally taboo as the word incest to many people. But it's also important if you want your back to get better and if you want to control your own time.

The trick is to practice and create new habits. That's why you're going to consistently say no to all inquiries that won't get you punched in the face or fired from work. To change a behaviour, you have to be hard on yourself, and not pick and choose what you're going to say no to. Say no to everything.

Be polite but determined. Come up with silly excuses ("I can't because I'm going to record a single with Adele") if you have to, but even better, say "I'm really sorry, but I can't". You'll discover that people like you even if you're not on their beck and call 24 hours a day.

Write down your challenge somewhere, together with your motivation, obstacles and strategies to overcome those obstacles.

Then, tell a few people you know about this challenge. The more open you are, the easier it will be. Especially if you ask those people to support you in case you relapse. Keep in contact with these people (it could be over the internet, too), and let them know how you're doing. Reward yourself every time you succeed. If you do fail once, think about why and find a new plan to succeed next time.

Once you've made it through these 30 days, you're much more likely to break the habit of always saying "yes". Do the same thing for every habit you want to break.

Tell the world how you did on my website:

http://www.ryggvarksexperternaljuger.se. For more tips on how to change your habits, check out this blog:

http://my-bad-habits.blogspot.com/.

With this boulder gone, you have an even greater chance to change your life, and we can now start having a look at the lies of back experts.

Lie 1: ”You have this diagnosis!”

How the answer creates the problem

The Dream Scenario

This has actually happened to me: The door opened and a very large lorry driver in his fifties entered, and he was quite uncomfortable being there, as most men his age are.

”I can barely walk”, he said, and that much I’d understood. I asked him to sit down so that I could examine him. He was convinced that it must be cancer or a severe hernia (maybe both!) and wanted surgery. Usually, patients think it takes too long to find out what they are suffering from, but this time it literally took less than 10 seconds to make a professional guess: Piriformis syndrome – and I saw that by looking at his wallet! I told him what I believed and said that I planned a more thorough examination, so if he could turn around, pull his trousers down and...

At this point he became very rigid, and I could tell he was going to need a short demonstration. He jumped almost half a meter and screamed. I apologized and said that it *was* Piriformis syndrome.

”I haven’t been able to sit properly for two weeks. Make sure you fix this. Send me to an orthopaedist or someone who can operate on me, preferably today, so that I can get rid of this tumour or whatever it is.”

”That won’t be needed. Get your wallet out.”

”Do you really think that I’m going to pay for this...”

I gestured for him to calm down and showed him my own wallet.

”Put the wallet *next to you* in the lorry, instead of sitting on it. With this beast in your back pocket, your bum cheeks will have a height difference of 5 centimetres. That’s why you’re in pain. You don’t need to have surgery. Just take this out and stretch your bum a little.”

He stared, ”How did you find out that quickly?”

I got up to show him that the conversation was over and said:

"One of the first things you learn in medicine is an old saying: *"When you hear hoof beats, think horses, not zebras."* In other words, take the simplest, most common and probable cause first.[8] Although you have a sedentary job, you do get a little exercise, you wouldn't suddenly be in pain *and* you have forced down a smaller hand bag in your back pocket. It was pretty simple. Besides, I have one lorry driver come in every week with the same problem..."

Unfortunately, it's not always that easy to determine the diagnosis.

You get the wrong diagnosis

> *Diagnosis – from "diá" (Greek, 'through, thoroughly') and "gignóskein" (Greek, 'to learn'), "to get to know thoroughly"*

Most diagnoses given by back experts are incorrect!

Not only that: Back experts know they're incorrect and do nothing about it.

If you think that sounds bad, just think about the repercussions: incorrect diagnoses mean incorrect prescriptions. When the patients are sent to water aerobics instead of surgery or have surgery instead of learning how to lift properly, this leads to increased costs for the entire health care system. If you don't care about that, then think about what it means for you: unnecessary suffering, more visits with the same back expert (or several) and secondary health problems.

We can agree that that's a bad thing, right?

It can seem strange that back experts are so poor at determining the correct diagnosis. Myself, I've had hour after hour of teaching how to make an accurate diagnosis. Most exams at the Karolinska Institute are about symptoms and diagnoses. There's hardly a shortage of material in the topic. The TV show "House" is even about a doctor that's an expert at making diagnoses.

In actual fact, this is the reason why so many diagnoses end up being incorrect. There's a huge pressure on back experts to determine

8 The method is also known as Occam's razor, attributed to William of Ockham, a philosopher from the 1300s.

a diagnosis. Both the system and the patients almost demand it. To the system, it's about placing the patient in the right compartment so that the accounting adds up.

The patient wants to know too. For many patients, the actual point of going to see an expert is to get a diagnosis, to know why they are in pain.

It may be unfortunate to find out that you have a hernia or that you need surgery – but at least that beats the insecurity of not knowing. Once you know, you can start planning for the rest of your life. And, you have something to tell your family and relatives who are wondering why things aren't like they usually are.

The education, the colleagues and the patients' expectations have created a kind of taboo. No back expert with any kind of self-respect would ever say: "*I don't know why you are in pain*". It's an iniquity to not know what the problem is. There are many alternatives to saying that you don't know. Vague umbrella terms are used for many ailments or terms that could be interpreted in several ways. Especially if they believe that the patient won't check the facts. Why not just tell the patient something, so they can get their diagnosis and go home and say "I have degenerative changes in my discs" instead of letting them walk around wondering?[9]

Never before have thousands of back experts been this irresponsible.

The easiest answer for a back expert is to look at malformations. If one of your vertebras look a little odd, or if one shoulder is higher than the other – then this will immediately be pointed out as the cause for your pain. In reality, this doesn't have to be the reason at all. Malformations or other deformities rarely have anything to do with the pain but are often blamed when the back experts are looking for a way to not say "I don't know".

The truth is that closer to 9 out of 10 people with back pain never find out the actual cause for their pain. Only one out of ten actually find out! Do you think you're one of them?

9 "Degenerative" means "worn out", but in health care, we don't like to say "worn out" since this worries patients, which increases their experience of pain.

Why do so few get the right diagnosis?

The reason why so few ever get the right diagnosis should be obvious, but naturally for most people it isn't:

The back is complex with many different parts and functions. The neck for example is one of the body's most movable joints (it can turn and bend considerably), while at the same time containing the vital connections between torso and head. Combined, the back is made up of 33 vertebras, which in turn contain spinal cords, the connection between the brain and the lower part of the body which is very sensitive as well as several large and strong muscle groups. The back is meant to balance your entire upper body while at the same time being the centre of all other movement. For example, think about how your back is working when you stretch for a cup of coffee on the table in front of you. Several muscle groups are involved, the spine is slightly twisted and your neck and head will most likely be affected so your balance will change. Then imagine how many movements like this you do every day, how many days you've been alive and how little you do to keep your back healthy.

The back is large, too complex and too active for it to be easy to provide simple answers.

You're being pigeonholed

Everyone wants to make things simple for themselves. Back experts are no exception. We like simple cases where we can make a diagnosis and give treatment so that you can make a full recovery. Like they say in American criminal dramas: "Open and shut case", which essentially means that you barely have time to start the examination before it's time to wrap it up.

For the police, this often means that someone in the family committed the crime so that they aren't required to search for other potential suspects. Us, back experts use diagnoses to compartmentalize you instead. It increases our chances for you to be an "open and shut case". We usually categorize patients with back pain in four different groups:

1. Weak back - often due to living a passive life or being overweight
2. Lower back pain – often caused by sudden, unfamiliar movements
3. The Sciatic nerve – the nerve is pinched
4. Lumbago-Sciatica – combines 2 and 3

Naturally, back experts realize that your back is more complex than that and they don't want to underplay your pain, but when you see a lot of suffering like we do, you have to organise it so that you can work more efficiently. It's a pure 80/20 way of thinking that makes it possible to categorize these problems.

The problem is that many people don't fit into any one of these categories – or they fit into all of them. That makes things confusing, and there are no easy answers.

That's why it's a good idea to not get worked up. The diagnosis could be important, but in most cases, it works out over time. The majority of people with back problems get rid of the pain in less than a week. So why get so worked up about it? Most likely, it will be enough to take a pain killer and maybe get a massage. A good book, a cup of hot chocolate and some caring words are never wrong either.

Diagnoses give you funny ideas

There's one big reason why back experts should avoid giving you a direct diagnosis:

Sometimes the problem sounds more serious than it is. Other times, it may sound minor, but in actuality it's major. The names are often misleading and us, back experts don't always understand how you interpret what we say. Maybe the most obvious example of this was when a doctor said that the test was positive. You're thinking "Hurray!", until someone explains that it may not be a positive thing after all. You may think you know what the diagnosis means. It's *not* guaranteed that you do.

Besides, the diagnosis will most likely make you an amateur

doctor. When you find out what you're suffering from, you start preparing to fix it yourself. You think that you know how to fix the problem. And, it most certainly is not an easy thing to do. If you for example find out that you've strained your back, you're likely to think that rest is the way to recover. That may not necessarily be the case! After all, there's a reason why we spend years in University.

If you really want to get rid of your back pain, there's a lot you can do once you've gotten a diagnosis. Ask us to explain, so that you fully understand what you're suffering from. It's not any stranger than reading the content label of the food you buy.

After that, it would be decent of you to give us a little time to find the right form of treatment. Preferably *before* you've made an appointment at *The comfy sofa's spa & relax.*

You may not need a diagnosis

Even if you most likely don't need a diagnosis because you're back will heal on its own, it could be that you're one of the few that really need one. To find out if you need a diagnosis, there are a few things you should keep your eyes open for:

1. The problems are reoccurring, even though you've done what you should, exercised regularly, spent less time sitting still and hunched over and are carrying around a little less weight.

2. You have one of the following "red flags":

- are under 18 years old
- have severe pain or an ache that started around the age of 50-60 years old
- an accident caused your pain
- continuous or increasing pain at night
- have previously had cancer
- are receiving steroid treatment for allergies
- are abusing drugs

- have HIV
- are losing a lot of weight
- are feeling generally exhausted
- always have difficulty moving
- feel pain at the slightest movement
- have a crooked back or other deformities
- have difficulty going to the toilet, controlling your urination or lose feeling in your nether regions.
- are having more and more difficulty walking and moving
- are very stiff in the mornings
- are having pain in your legs and/or arms
- have annoying skin rashes, colitis or incontinence
- have relatives with back problems[10]

If you're experiencing any of these symptoms, see a doctor immediately!

But there could also be less urgent reasons for getting a diagnosis. That's why we're going to continue as if nothing has happened.

You should get more than one diagnosis

In case your back pain is reoccurring or continuous, the chances are that you are suffering from more than one thing.

As I just said, the body is able to heal most minor injuries on its own. Most doctors agree that a large part of the job is doing as little as possible while the body is handling it.

But every now and then, a situation comes up when not just one thing happens, but several things collide. You may have slept poorly, are feeling tense and lift something heavy. The body struggles with these things. It struggles with choosing what to prioritize and heal first. The body especially struggles with healing things that complete

10 "Degenerative" means "worn out", but in health care, we don't like to say "worn out" since this worries patients, which increases their experience of pain.

other things, for example if you're in pain both when you're resting and making an effort.

If you see a back expert for continuous or reoccurring problems, you should be suspicious if you only get one diagnosis. If the back expert claims that your issues are related to lifting wrong, then you should be sceptical. Your body can heal that on its own.

You can make it easier for your back expert to see the different diagnoses by describing your problems in as much detail as you can. Back experts listen properly and then make their judgement depending on what you say.

A large problem with long-lasting, continuous pain is that it can move. A lot of patients recover from the symptoms they first came to get help for, to then notice that they're hurting in a different area. This kind of pain is not just frustrating for the patient and the back expert, but it's also tricky to find the real cause for. Back experts realize their limitations if they've fixed two kinds of pain and the pain moved to another area of the body. Instead of continuing to see the patient, they should send you to a different clinic with more resources and where they have experience in this kind of situation. If the pain continues during a long period of time, and no physical cause can be found, then you have to start looking for something in the patient's personality or emotional life that could be behind it. The connection between body and soul will be discussed more further on.

How you get a good diagnosis

My advice to the people who need a diagnosis: Aim for a good diagnosis. Not a bad one, but a good one.

Before you say "Thank you, Captain Brilliant!" I'd like to add how you know if a diagnosis is good.

To make a diagnosis takes time.

If the examination takes less than twenty seconds (and you're not carrying a purse in your back pocket, as the lorry driver did), you can assume that the quality will be about the same. You might as well read the truth of that miracle treatment in the evening paper's health section.

The back expert is asking you questions.

And you get to answer them. And the back expert seems to be listening. Making notes is an individual thing and is not a base for how well he or she is listening. At the very least, the back expert should not only read your records, but also confirm that what it says is correct. Common questions are often regarding how your back pain started, any previous pain and how your life situation is looking.

The two most important conclusions that a back expert is trying to make are:

1) if the problem has to do with the spine or not

2) if the problem is caused by a serious illness or not[11]

Again, how accurate the diagnosis is depends on you. If you reply to the questions in a way that can be interpreted in different ways, the back expert will assume that you mean the "regular" of the two. The most common explanation may not be accurate in your case, but the back expert can't know that, that's why it's important that you reply as clearly as you can. In Part 4 you can find information on how to prepare for your appointment.

The back expert does a manual examination.

This involves feeling your back and asking you to execute certain movements. The idea is among other things to see the limits of your pain, and if there are any obvious causes, such as marks or deformities. The back expert will also try to exclude the most common problems.

11 Merck's manuals online have a good overview of how a diagnosis is determined: https://tinyurl.se/backpain

Sometimes the back expert will take an x-ray image and/or an ultrasound or other tests.

There are a lot of different types of tests: ordinary x-rays, MRI, contrast x-ray (myelography or discography), CT scans, ultrasound or blood tests. To go through any of these tests isn't something to strive for. There's no point to it. On the contrary, this kind of "proof" could give you funny ideas. Really, you need a proper education to read them correctly. It looks simpler than it is.

The back expert should not give you a diagnosis before that.

He or she could tell you about possible causes during the examination, but the final diagnosis should be determined at the end of the process.

The explanation should make sense. If anything is unclear, ask the back expert to show you the problem on a skeleton or a picture.

If despite everything, the diagnosis is "I don't know" once the examination is finished, it doesn't mean that's a weakness. On the other hand, it's a sign that you have a back expert you should hold on to. Back pain is very difficult to diagnose and it's often better to have further examinations done than get the wrong diagnosis.

When you receive your diagnosis from your back expert, challenge him or her with questions:

* "How did you come to this conclusion?"
* "How serious is it?"
* "Will I make a full recovery?"
* "Are there any other possible causes?"
* "What can I do to speed up my recovery?"

By doing this, you will get an increased understanding of your problems while you at the same time establish that your back expert is an individual person who is taking responsibility for your back and not just any sketchy type. Good back experts will respect this and see it as an assent in the fight to become pain free.

Lie 2: "You'll be pain free in 5 minutes!"

MIRACLES HAPPEN IMMEDIATELY. WONDERS TAKE A LITTLE LONGER.

"The person who doesn't believe in miracles is not a realist. But the one who builds their existence on miracles is a fool."

– *ROLF BIGLER (1930-1978), SWISS JOURNALIST AND AUTHOR.*

"Everyone thinks of changing the world, but no one thinks of changing himself."

– *LEO TOLSTOY (1828-1910), RUSSIAN AUTHOR IN "PAMPHLETS" (1900)*

"The million-dollar roll"

an exclusive wellness facility, London, 2002

We were 12 back experts, each one of us with their own examination room. I had yet to become used to it, so I spent a lot of my time studying the others.

In the room next to me, Steve had his work place. He was just over 50 years old, dressed in an Armani suit, had a large Rolex made in gold on his wrist and almost looked like Richard Gere. I used to call him the "Golden Boy". He was always talking and charming everyone.

One day, we were sitting in his examination room. It was decorated with designer furniture and gold. Even the steel around the treatment table was in gold. I've never seen anything close to it before. There and then, I told him that I, myself was experiencing back pain.

He smiled widely. "Let my magic hands fix the problem!" he said and instructed me to lie down on the golden bed. Without asking any questions, and without me having shown him where the pain was located, we heard a loud crack! It came from my back!

After the treatment we went and had lunch. Sure enough, my back felt better. I was surprised. What happened?

When we came back and started seeing patients again, I saw him enter his room with his first patient. Through the wall I could hear Golden Boy's smooth words. He told his patient that it would only take 10 visits, and after that she would be fully recovered. In my room, I saw a patient with very severe pack pain and I estimated that it would take longer. Suddenly, I felt like an amateur.

That feeling quickly disappeared. As I kept hearing Steven's patients through the thin walls, I realised that he has a well-practised script for each one of the ten times. He told all the patients the same thing. Each one of them went ten times. At the end of it, they all received the same crack, I had that first time.

I later found out from another back expert, that that crack was called "*the million-dollar roll*".[12] The reason for that was because everyone bought it. The loud crack sounds very convincing. Even I bought into it. But probably, the placebo effect is behind a large part of the success. That's why some back experts use nut shells that they step on or other things like it to create a loud cracking sound.

Steven was fully booked, month after month. It wasn't the nice schools he had attended, nor the awards he had received that were the cause. His success was based on him convincing his patients that all they needed was for him to create a cracking sound from their backs.

The fact remains, that there are times when it's okay to do "the million-dollar roll". It's a generic technique that increases mobility. I've used it too and will use it in the future. But, I will never do what Steven did, and use it on all of my patients, no matter how much money I could make. There are certain risks with the technique if you're not careful.

In summary: I use "the million-dollar roll" when a patient could benefit from it. I never use it otherwise. That's what every sensible back expert does.

12 https://www.chiroweb.com/mpacms/dc_ca/article.php?id=38313

A full recovery could take time

If you're in enough pain for it to last so long that you have time to tough it out a day or so before making an appointment to see a back expert, then something is causing that pain. As we found out in the last chapter, it's not that simple to find the cause. But one thing is for sure:

> *It will take longer than 5 minutes before you're free from pain! And it will take time before you can move like you normally would.*

Why?

Because, you can't always cure *X* by taking pill *Y* or doing exercise *Z*. It's not even a guarantee that you will fully recover. Just because you know what you're suffering from, doesn't mean that you can find a way to ease it. Unfortunately, the truth is that you can't always know if something can be done against the pain or not.

But most importantly: even if you're lucky enough that a back expert can give you a diagnosis and recommend a form of treatment that will actually help, it can still take a long time before you make a full recovery. We may even speak about months or years.

In part 4 (starting on page 164), there's a chapter on how you can live with back pain. It may be a comfort to know that there are options, even if your recovery is not as quick as you would've liked.

Why do they let you think it takes 5 minutes?

Deep down, you also know that it takes more than 5 minutes to make a full recovery, but considering how excruciating it is, you're hoping to find that short cut that will lead directly to a pain free life. But what if... there's a universal cure that could solve your problem.

It's called magic thinking.

Evening papers, health magazines, weekly magazines and popular scientific papers know that you think this way, and both quacks and bad back experts use this to their advantage. They're making money off of confirming your hopes that there is a quick fix, or that "the scientists are working on a new miracle cure". They know that you'll book up all the appointments and buy all their products – just like the Golden Boy's patients – because they're telling you that it works and won't take long before you're fully recovered.

The bitter reality on the other hand, is not as easy to sell. Especially not since you've seen tons of films and TV programs where the problems are fixed in an hour or two. If you think that I'm exaggerating regarding Hollywood's influence, then I can refer you to the examinations that show that even you believe that good looking people are smarter and more successful, because that's the way it is on film.[13]

Back pain should be curable in five minutes, but it's not. I know that it's not what you want to hear, but I'd rather be honest with you and that means you may be forced to deal with the pain and the decreased mobility. You have the right to know the situation. You should demand the same thing from your back expert.

In my eyes, this is about how to manage important information. If you claim that it's possible to become pain free in five minutes, you are withholding important information, maybe so that the patient can live in a dream world. But more likely, it's because you can earn money because of it.

All the back experts that know what you're thinking and continue to let you live in that lie, or possibly even feed you that lie are not just greedy. They're dangerous! They're willing to do things like "the million-dollar roll" even when it's not necessary and that could cause you harm.

You should get a reasonable recovery period

To try to rush your body's recovery is neither easy nor wise. When you take short cuts, the risk is that you do too much too early and your pain comes back, probably worse than before. It's better to fully recover first.

That's why, you should be very suspicious if your back expert

13 www.hofstra.edu/pdf/orsp_shahanidenning_spring03.pdf as well as Richard Wiseman Quirkology: The Curious Science of Everyday Lives, Basic Books, 2008, Chapter 4

says that he can fix it during one visit. The odds are quite small that these kinds of tricks are successful, and on the contrary, it's likely that your back expert is counting on the placebo effect to make you feel "healed".

That is, healed enough to be impressed, but not pain free enough to not come back for another visit.

I consider that kind of behaviour to be the same kind of false marketing as what the phone sales people do, where they lure you in with a 1-pound promise just to trick you. The real cost is much higher. If you during the first visit at the clinic is somehow told that you'll need exactly one visit, then you may buy into it because of the price – even though the real price is much higher.

Other back experts use another kind of hoax, the same one Golden Boy used above, to give a precise answer. Sorry, it's not possible to give any general rules for exactly how long it "should" take. That's the actual point. If your back expert says that it will take (more or less) six or 12 times, then it may be time for you to think about how your back expert could possibly know that. Do you have a back that is better or worse than expected?

A decent back expert never leaves immediate answers of whether or not you'll be fully recovered. He or she can on the other hand say something along the lines of: "These kinds of injuries *usually* take a month or two to heal."

The back expert should receive bonus points if he or she follows up with: "What do you think about us booking you in for 6-8 visits and then we'll evaluate if my treatment is helping you? If it isn't having the desired effect, I will refer you to someone I believe can help."

By scaling down their own role and participation and thereby focusing on your body's healing abilities, that back expert has shown you real concern.

Someone may ask if this doesn't wear on your self-confidence, to fail to help your patients. But when you've worked with this for a while, you realise that you can't heal everyone. Often, the best thing you can do is to make sure that the patient gets to see an expert within the area of the main issue. Many patients feel disappointed, and I can understand that: they waited for a long time to get an appointment, they're in pain and they're frustrated. That's when it's more important than ever to not just do things to please the patient. I meet many patients that have jumped between physiotherapists, naprapaths, chiropractors, massage therapists and so on, without improving because no one has been honest and sent them to a neurologist for example, who is far more competent in the area than I am. You can't have that kind of prestige.

Pain free quickly – for real!

In many cases it is possible to become pain free quickly, I don't deny that. I just want to prepare you, because it *could* take longer than five minutes. Sometimes it takes a lot longer than five minutes. But that's not a reason to start looking for a cure in the wrong places. The cure is usually a lot closer than you think. You don't even need a back expert. There's a lot you can do yourself to become pain free.

First of all: Don't worry! Bad back pain normally disappears within a few days to a few months, and 90 percent of everyone who are experiencing acute problems in their lower back can return to normal activities within four weeks. Only one out of 200 cases of back pain are caused by dangerous medical conditions. Back pain is rarely life threatening. The calmer you are, the quicker you will recover. There are even scientists that say that negative thoughts increase the level of pain we feel.[14]

The next step is easy. *Take a pain killer* with anti-inflammatory properties. Over the counter medicine such as Ibuprofen and Paracetamol works well for treatment of light to medium symptoms.

A lot of people like to have *cold- or hot packs* or both. If so, begin with cold. Place ice-cubes or similar in a bag or towel – never directly against the skin. The ice reduces inflammation and ”slows down” the nerves, which eases the pain. You should only use cold for 20-30-minute intervals.

Heat on the other hand works best after the first 48 hours. The heat widens the blood vessels, so more blood can reach the area and heal the injury. You can for example heat a damp towel in the

14 The scientists Ronald Melzack and Patrick David Well wrote about "the gate control" theory as early as 1964 in "Pain mechanisms – a new theory", http://www.ncbi.nlm.nih.gov/pubmed/5320816

microwave oven, but only use the towel for about 20 minutes per hour. Be careful to not burn yourself.[15]

Support in the form of a corset, pillows or bandages can help to increase the stability for your back. This is usually very appreciated. Especially so by the people who manage to hide that they're wearing a corset. It sculptures the waist nicely. But all types of support should only be used during shorter periods of time so that your body gets used to doing the work by itself.

15 Loïc Burn, Michael S. Sinel, William W. Deadorff *Treating your back & neck pain for dummies* (2007), John Wiley & Sons, kapitel 6

Inconvenient Back Challenge Nr. 4

When you've suffered from back pain for a while, even your friends and family start to get tired of the complaints. It's human to complain, but it won't make things better. To remove the fourth boulder that makes it more difficult for your back to recover, you have to learn how to stop complaining.

How you express yourself is a clear sign of how you see yourself. If you complain, you probably see yourself as a victim. People who see themselves as victims notice fewer opportunities, and it therefore becomes more difficult to get out of a bad situation.

The solution is not to pretend that everything is fine. You have to be able to express your feelings. The problem comes about when the complaining becomes a pattern: constant bullshit about others, "feel-sorry-for-me"-urges and negative thoughts about most things.

You can decide to change this and become healthier at the same time. Decide to stop complaining for three weeks. No complaints at all during this time. Wear a bracelet on one arm – and if you or anyone else catches you complaining, move the bracelet to the other arm and start over. Do this openly if you can (see challenge 3) and tell your surroundings how you're doing. Maybe others will join you. If you discover that someone else is complaining and point it out, not only that person, buy you, too should move the bracelet.

Be ready for this to take time. 21 days in a row without complaining is difficult. It could take anywhere between four to eight months to succeed.

Lie 3: "Exercise yourself healthy"

WHY YOU SHOULD TAKE A LOOK AT EXERCISES YOU SHOULDN'T DO

"You can't tell a kid that it's time to exercise; that's a turn-off... You have to say "Let's go to the park and have some fun." Then you can get them to do some running, play on the swings, practice on the balance beam, basically get a full workout disguised as play."

– Arnold Schwarzenegger (born 1947), Austrian "actor" and former American governor

"The best exercise is the one you actually do."

– unknown, sometimes accredited to Stephan Rössner, professor and physician at the department of medicine at the Karolinska university hospital

You get too many exercises

When you leave the back expert, you've probably got a whole load of exercises that you should be doing. You may feel a little hesitant to these exercises and you're wondering whether you should be doing them or not.

You're not the only one. The back expert knows that you won't be doing the exercises. The reason is simple: The back expert himself wouldn't be doing them either!

In other words, both the patient and the back expert have lied to each other: "Will you be doing these exercises?" "Yes, of course."

These kinds of pointless conversations eat up a lot of time. To explain and demonstrate, and to learn the exercises take up very much time for very little results. That time could have been spent on things that matter. The next patient could've been seen and treated.

Imagine yourself sitting in the waiting room waiting for patients that only come in to exchange pleasantries with your back expert. Wouldn't you rather have wanted that patient to let you go and see your back expert instead?

Here's a small mathematical exercise: Multiply how much time is spent on appointments with the number of patients each back expert has. Then multiply that number with the number of back experts and you'll get a whole lot of wasted time. I calculated this and double checked it, and when the number was still the same, I phoned up a colleague to triple check my calculations. His reaction was: "I don't know if I should laugh or cry." The number of hours back experts spend on giving exercises that no one is planning on doing is almost *forty times as many* as us Swedes spend on watching the weather reports and then complaining about it in a year! *Forty times*![16]

No wonder the waiting lines for treatment are so long.

Many back experts seem to think that patients don't have a life beyond their back pain, but want to do exercises all day long. They seem to think that with more exercises, the chances are bigger that some of them will help.

And that they do. I usually accept patients that are suffering from back pain from carrying bags full of exercise instructions.

16 Actually, that's not true. I'm lying. There are no such numbers available. But the point is worth taking seriously. Just do the exercises we give you already!

The problem is really quite serious. The more exercises you get, the bigger the chances are that you won't do them. The same goes if the exercises are meant be done too often. You always miss one exercise opportunity and that quickly goes from a first sin to more. Pretty soon the whole exercise program has been thrown off the ship like a bad fish.

By doing this the back expert hasn't only turned the patient into a lazy person with bad conscience, but he or she has also created an image of back experts as people who have unrealistic expectations and no real idea of what the patients are doing.

When you receive exercises from a back expert, it's easy to get pulled into the "sure, I'll follow all the instructions I've been given" – mentality. Try to take a step back and think about it. Will you really follow the program or is it building unrealistic expectations. Compare with how much you usually work out. If you don't exercise regularly, maybe you can think of other things you do several times a week, for example hobby projects or visiting friends. The whole question can be summarised like this:

Are you bull headed enough to do the exercises during week three, when you've lost the initial motivation, when things are starting to get in the way and you feel that you've improved enough to maybe give it up?

You get the wrong exercises

Flip through the pages of any of the thousands of books on how to get rid of back pain. Each one of them have exercises. A lot of exercises. You'll find lots of exercises online too. I'm sure I could gather several hundreds of exercises, only from the books I have in my reception.

The access to the exercises isn't the problem.

But not all exercises are created equally. A lot of them are actually quite meek. Some of them don't do very much. Others have shown to be wrong for certain types of patients.

There's a pretty big risk that you'll be given the wrong exercises – for you. That's right, the exercises have to be adjusted to you as an individual. The exercises that work for you could be harmful or useless to your colleague. Or the other way around, of course.

If you give yourself the exercises it increases the chances that they're not right for you since you most likely lack the competence needed to determine what exercises are right for you. The exercises you're given by back experts aren't necessarily much better. Many back experts choose the same exercises out of routine since it saves time. They pick the same pamphlet or put the patient in the same positions as they usually do and give them the same speech they've done a hundred times before that.

It's hard to find such poor treatment. Talk about not seeing the patient as an individual person. I can imagine that a lot of them complain about others having treated them the same way: parking guards that follow the rules, the insurance company with their regulations and the children's teacher who can't see their kids among all the other children.

If you receive a copied booklet or a printed pamphlet, this is a clear warning signal, but wait to see if the back expert marks out any exercises you should do. There should be some exercises you *shouldn't* be doing in the collection.

It's harder to judge if the back expert gives you a ”one size fits all” or if it's a customized version if he or she only shows you the exercises you need to do (without giving you any printed material). You can always ask or confront us. You could for example say: “Is this an exercise you're giving for all kinds of back pain?” The answer should be ”no”, ”nope” or ”You've read Robin Wakeham's book, haven't you?”.

No matter what kind of exercises you're given, there's an important point here: Almost all kinds of movement is better than sitting still, but specific problems are best solved with specific exercises. To have the energy and motivation to do the exercises that have been specifically picked for you, it's important that you ignore all other exercises and that you understand why you're doing exactly those exercises! That's right, ignore the ones that have nothing to do with it.

What should you do to get rid of your back pain?

You've probably already heard or read my first three tips on how to get rid of back pain. That's no coincidence. In most cases, those three tips are all you need. Sometimes you may need some methods with a little sting to them. You'll find those after the first three methods.

1. The first and probably most common tip is to *get into the habit of taking walks*. This is one of the most underestimated cures for back pain, maybe because it's free and seems too easy. Okay, if it's that easy, do it then! I believe that you could take a walk but getting into the habit of taking walks several times a week is more difficult than a lot of other options. But not impossible. Start by:

- Decide a destination or a specific route rather than wandering aimlessly. The route should be long enough and the destination far enough so that you get approximately an hour's worth of walking. You walk around 4-6 kilometres per hour (more if you crank it up), which means that you should choose a place that's 2-3 kilometres away or take a route for at least 5 kilometres. If you're lacking imagination, search for "walks" in your area on the internet.
- Take the same walk each time, bring music or a friend and write it down in the calendar.
- Wear good shoes, dress according to the weather and stand outside your door. Stay there. Rub your hands together or smile expectantly – or whatever you do to show that something fun is about to happen. Do this whether you think so or not. You're in the process of teaching yourself that walks are nice and fun.
- After that, you can start walking. Walk at your own pace. Try to avoid limping or walking carefully.
- If you can, avoid hills and sloping roads as much as possible.
- Look at your surroundings
- When you get there, smile! Really smile!
- Back home: Write down your next walk in the calendar, no

more than three days later.

* Start counting down the days to your next walk.
* If you can, make plans with someone you know that can come with you for the next walk. Start the conversation by suggesting a place that you both may be interested in.

2. If it doesn't work, *see a back expert.* He or she can recommend good exercises for your type of back pain (as long as you watch out for back experts that give too many exercises, or all of them). Do this:
* Find your doctor's number. It's most likely among the bills or on the counter. Book an appointment.

* Explain what kind of back pain you are having with the help of the tips on page 228.
* If the doctor considers your back pain to be severe, you will be referred to a back expert.
* When you see the back expert, ask about exercises and show that you're ready to make an effort.
* It may be obvious but *follow the recommendations*.
* Don't stop just because you feel a little better.
* Keep doing the exercises or similar exercises.
* Keep going.
* Keep going... The secret lies in doing the exercises for a long period of time. You don't need to stop because your back is improving. On the contrary, it's a good habit.

3. If you want to recover quicker, you can also *start weight lifting* in combination with your exercises. You need the strength and flexibility. And, it's fun. Do this:

* You don't need a personal trainer or a gym membership to some trendy place. You can do it at home, at work or at a regular gym. Don't look for excuses, just get started.
* Set aside time from the beginning. Preferably from your TV-

time or time you spend on magazines, time sitting and talking to your partner (you may as well do that on a spinning bike or on a workout mat), or time where you don't really do anything special. If you've done a 80/20 analysis, you know there's plenty of time.

* Spend as little time as possible on getting the right equipment – only the bare essentials and even then, less is better. You don't even need workout clothes.
* Smile before you get started, stop for a moment during the exercise and smile and smile when you're done. Or laugh – it's up to you. You need all the "feel-good" hormones you can get.
* Use music or company or absolute calm to make time go faster.
* Count down the reps from 30.
* Keep going even after 30 times. Do that by smiling or laughing even more.
* Keep doing this your whole life!

I'm not going to introduce a bunch of exercises with images and descriptions here. It's not because I don't think it's important. Exercise is proven to be effective. Start now! You'll find more tips as usual in part 4, on page Error: The source could not be found.

You already know this. And the exercises are available in so many other books and online. It would be disrespectful of me to spend a lot of time on things you already know. It would just waste your time.

Go through the first three steps properly. If they're not working and you're being completely honest with yourself, move on to the next two steps:

4. *Think positive.* It may even sound more cliché than the previous tips, and I know that there's a lot of cheerful, plasticky literature that preaches: "Don't worry, be happy". I also know how many gurus there are out there that claim that they can solve any problem in 30 days if you follow their method; which is to be an optimist. There are also a lot of books about how misled people have been by the ruthless belief that everything will be okay.[17]

17 http://www.barbaraehrenreich.com/brightsided.htm

But, just like the three steps above, this is something you know you should do because you know it works, but that you aren't doing. To see the future and feel hope is proven to be effective. To have fun both decreases pain and is nice. One common example is of the case of Norman Cousins, a journalist that was diagnosed with a heart problem, but realized that the doctors could only do 50% of the work. The rest was up to him. That's why he checked in to a hotel and watched clips of the Marx Brothers. 10 minute-videos gave him 2 hours with no pain.[18]

But there are a lot of other people who have researched the same thing, especially sports psychologists that say that it's important to visualize positive outcomes. It trains the brain to be successful. You don't need to be the best in the world nor a district champion or deny negative things – you just need to choose to see that there is a lot that you can do. Choose to smile, choose to hope. If you're going to keep your motivation up, it's also important that you like what you're doing. Whether you're doing something you like or are learning to like what you're doing so that the result will be that you're doing something you like. [19]

The fifth and last step is for those of you who have done the previous four steps: taken walks, done the exercises you've been given by your back expert, been weightlifting and thinking positive. If you've already gone through these steps and suspect that your mind is in imbalance which is leading to you physically hurting, then this is the step for you.

After this, there aren't any more steps. That is because you don't need any more steps after this:

5. If everything else fails, and you're still in pain after trying these methods for six months and you haven't received a diagnosis that explains why you are in pain, then it's time to try something new and to think bigger. The solution is to look elsewhere. *Your problem may not be your back or even your body.*

The body is affected by feelings (step 4), but also by more

18 Norman Cousins, Anatomy of an illness as perceived by the patient: reflections on healing (Norton, 1979)

19 S. Lyobomirsky, L.A. King, och E. Diener "The benefits of frequent positive effect: does happiness lead to success?" (Psychological Bulletin, nr 131, 205, s 80355), cited in Richard Wiseman 59 seconds, Macmillan 2009, Chapter "Happiness

permanent psychological states: difficulties letting go, being passive aggressive, suffering from inferiority complex or other problems. After eliminating the body as a cause, and you're still suffering from back pain, the cause for your problems is most likely in your personality or your background.

Your symptoms are real and so is your pain, but there isn't a physical reason behind the pain. I want to emphasize that I do understand that you aren't lying. And it's nothing to be ashamed of: No one thinks you need to spend time in a mental institution. You're in pain and that's something you need help with. And you will get help, you just need to let people help you. Do this:

> * To admit that you're having a spiritual problem is for many people a much bigger step than admitting a physical problem – and we all know how difficult *that* can be. But it's time to leave the safe but pain-inducing things and move on in life. You've tried the way you live now long enough and you're not getting all the things you should from life. Think about all the other times you've changed: you moved away from home, you got a job, you lost a job, things ended with your first love, you were in an accident and so on. You can go through the same kind of changes on your own, for example when you book a holiday (compare with my holiday on page 27). All of these changes start in your mind. Decide to admit that you have a problem, that you've collected certain emotional events/relationships – without specifying them. It's enough that you tell yourself that the problem is with you. (Or, if you're not quite there yet, admit that the problem *may* be with you.)

> * Write down the two-three feelings you struggle with the most. You may be worried, depressed, angry, stressed or have bad self-confidence. You already know these feelings. They're the ones you think "can't be helped" and that you are reluctant to do anything about. If you're finding this difficult to do, then one clue is to look at your biggest problems in life – what feelings do they stir in you? Not the feelings that everyday issues cause, but the really hard-to-solve, super serious problems that affect you. The uncomfortable feelings.

Don't try to solve them, just write them down. Maybe it's the first time you write them down?

* Look at the note with your feelings. These are your problems; not back pain or other symptoms you've had throughout the years (for example headaches or strong allergies). These are the feelings that are causing your back pain. You don't need to be afraid of the actual back pain. Isn't that a relief?

* By just finding these feelings, you've taken a big step. Celebrate it! Celebrate your "discovery" by doing something you like.

* Now the insight that it is your feelings that are the reason for your back pain needs to sink it. Your brain has created your pain to avoid dealing with the feelings and that's why you're experiencing all kinds of resistance to do something about it.

* The best way to do something about the inner resistance is to learn more about what happened. *I strongly recommend that you order or buy Dr Jogn E. Sarno's book Healing Back Pain (1991)* where he describes in more detail how your brain tries to protect you from the awful feelings and how it causes you pain. Sarno has saved thousands of people from back pain and goes deeper than any other (easy to access) book in the topic of stress-related backpain.[20] To buy *Healing Back Pain* may cost you 15-20 quid. You can afford that. Spend less money on crisps or that expensive work out equipment if you have to.

* Read the book and follow the recommendations!

* Convince yourself that the pain you feel isn't severe by focusing on the real causes (the ones you wrote down). The harder you focus on the actual problems and feelings, the less back pain you'll experience since the pain is no longer

20 https://www.spinehealth. com/conditions/depression/stressrelatedbackpain

needed.

Admit that you are angry, if that's how you feel. Bring out the worry properly, if those are your feelings. Let the low self-confidence speak. Look at the monster. Look at it carefully. That's when you'll realise that it isn't a monster. It's a part of you. It's a feeling, nothing more and nothing less.

* Feel your emotions! Let them out. The back pain will disappear pretty quickly.

* Talk to people about this. Let your family know that you're feeling stressed or that your self-confidence is low. If your family doesn't want to listen, speak to someone else: a work friend, a childhood friend, someone you met through your hobby, or someone you accidentally got stuck in a lift with. People will like you more, when they know about your "secret", not less. Because they've been shown trust, that's a gift.

Sarno's method is tried and very effective. There's one more thing to think about: When you've shown your feelings and your back pain has disappeared, there is a risk for it to come back in another part of your body.

See it for what it is: Your brain is trying to make you close your eyes to your real problems; your feelings and focus on the pain instead. But you know better: Feel the emotion and let it come up to the surface. It will make the pain go away.

The best exercises in the world

It's time to introduce the best exercises in the world! These exercises will change everything! You'll get rid of your pain and even prevent accidents and genetic deformities!

The greatness will start on the next page.

Before you move to the next page and your life changes forever, take a moment to think about what these exercises could be. Don't peek but use your imagination. How do you think the world's best exercises would look? And how would it feel to finally be free from pain? It's only a few seconds away now.

Take a deep breath, imagine it and how you're beginning to embrace the exercises in your life. You're already starting to feel how the pain is disappearing – that's how efficient the exercises are.

Okay, time to turn the page!

On the next page, you'll find the exercises that are the shortcut to a back free from pain!

There are no exercises that fix all problems!

All shortcuts to a pain free back are lies!

If you believed this lie you haven't read this book properly.

Put away this book and do something else! You're not committed enough to want to do anything about your back pain.

Wouldn't it be nice to not have to deal with all this responsibility that comes with reading this book? Don't you feel how you'd rather feel sorry for yourself for being in so much pain? Aren't you starting to feel tempted to find some back doctor who only gives the easy answers? My advice is to listen to those feelings. Put this book somewhere where someone who wants to do something about their back pain can find it.

Do something else instead. You're not going to follow the instructions, so save yourself and me a lot of time.

Is there anything good on TV maybe?

You still have the chance to live life as a normal person.

That's what you really want.

It's time to be honest with yourself.

Inconvenient Back Challenge Nr. 5

I'm not going to have a single specific exercise in this book. Seriously, don't you have enough information, exercises, equipment and so on?

If you're still disappointed, it's because you've failed to *do something for longer than 2 weeks*. You want someone to do the hard work for you. So, when that initial enthusiasm dies away, you stop – and then you've failed again. Next time will be more difficult, since you see yourself as someone who doesn't follow through on your projects.

You're not alone in this pattern. Whole industries to do with diets, exercise, personal development and so on thrive on you failing so that you can come back and pay new fees.

Isn't it time for you to change that? When you've learned how to, step by step, you will be able to remove another boulder from your backpack.

This is what you do to push on:

5. Choose a goal that is easily measured.

6. Write down the goal and put it somewhere visible!

7. Motivate yourself by a) writing down what you do and b) telling your surroundings what you're doing so that they can push and help you.[21] The motivation needs to be really strong, and that's when you should be looking at your 80/20 analysis.

8. Get a trigger, that is an activity that you already do and that comes just before the thing you should do. For example: every time you've brushed your teeth, you always take a walk. Connect these two things in your head.

9. Every time you miss two chances in a row, think about why and get another trigger: Rewards, pressure from your surroundings, whatever you need...

---

21 A blog that is good at writing about how you stay motivated is: http://zenhabits.net/top20motivationhacksoverviw//

More specifically: Get a spinning bike. On eBay and Gumtree there are close to thousands for sale, many below fifty quid. Make sure it has a comfortable saddle, and that you can use the pedals – otherwise, it doesn't need any other special stuff. Put the bike in front of the TV! Nowhere else. Then cycle every day for 20-25 minutes while you're watching Jerry Springer or Let's Dance or whatever it is you like to watch. There you have an easy goal and trigger.

If you have a hernia and can't cycle, go out and walk for 20-25 minutes! You can watch TV on your phone at the same time. (Don't even try it. I've heard every single excuse in the book.) Bike or walk – every day for 30 days.

Tell your friends what you're doing. Chances are that they'll say something condescending, but in secrecy they're jealous. Ask them to help you instead (Remember: Don't complain!), and make sure they hear how you're doing daily.

Start small and make sure the exercise routine is deeply rooted in your body for 1 year. When you've done that, move on to step 2, that is to sign up for one of the world's biggest challenges for motivated exercisers! For example, Run New York City Marathon, walk Spain's famous pilgrimage trail Camino De Santiago, climb to Mount Everest Base Camp, swim the English Channel or join the Ironman triathlon in China.

The majority of these races also have exercises on their websites with information that tell you exactly what you need to do every day to prepare for the challenge as well as forums and so on so that you can become part of the gang.

Besides decreased back pain and better health, you will also get new friends.

You can also download the book FYSS (Physical Activity in the Prevention and Treatment of Disease). This book is a collaboration between Swedish Professional Associations for Physical Activity (YFA) and Public Health Information. You can also buy the printed version through them for approximately 20 pounds. The book contains neutral information about exercise, so that you won't buy into all the latest trends and shams in exercise.

When you've been doing something for a year, chances are smaller that you'll quit.

Lie 5: ”It costs 5,000 quid to get better”

HOW THE BED BUSINESS RIPS YOU OFF BECAUSE YOU’RE DESPERATE

”What’s the secret, Robin?”

Cape town, South Africa, [2000]

I in the backseat of the UH-1 Huey-helicopter the sound of Lynard Skynard’s “Sweet home Alabama” was beaming from the speakers and competing against the deafening roar from the rotor – and maybe the adrenalin that was pumping through my body. We were jolted around by the half-crazed pilot.

I looked down on my uniform and felt like I was in a Vietnam war movie. Everyone were wearing full equipment and the ”enemy” had entrenched themselves a few minutes away.

That’s when I started to think about what an odd situation I was in. It was my first free trip. Considering the luxury I’d experienced, I was happy for the “all expenses paid” trip.

The day before we’d gone diving with sharks, and the day before that we’d sat in a Jeep and looked out over the savannah looking for ”the big five” – the five most difficult animals to hunt on foot: lion, leopard, African buffalo, African elephant and the black rhinoceros. Every night and a few of the days there were parties with expensive champagne and cigars. And now, an advanced war simulation with real Vietnam helicopters and full equipment.

The other men, because there were mostly men on the trip, were all over 50 years of age. They owned at least one bed store each, and some of them were in charge of complete bed store chains. Myself, I was a brat aged 33 who didn’t even have an actual physical store for my beds. And still, I’d sold many more than I should, more than most of them.

I got more than a few sharp looks and many questioning comments. They all wanted to know how I succeeded *without a physical store.* When they found out that I enjoyed vintage champagne, they thought it was my weak point and tried to get me drunk. But, when I'm in "enemy territory" with strangers that want my business secrets, I'm very careful with how much I drink and the old men left emptyhanded.

Yet, the secret was right in front of their eyes: I had a website where I had collected the best and most efficient products against pain in one place – with quick delivery. But, it wasn't my presence online that was crucial, even if it probably played a part since they thought the internet was mostly a hassle. No, the secret was simpler than that: They sold all kinds of beds. I had removed 80% of those that had nothing to do with pain and focused on the 20% that were left. People quickly understood that they should turn to me if they were in pain. Unlike their philosophy, where more was better, I felt that fewer were better, and I succeeded in topping their sales numbers after only *a year.*

And there, in the helicopter where the rock music and the sound of the rotor blades where lulling me into a strange calm, I understood *their* secret too*: The margins in the bed business are huge.* That's why there are all kinds of fortune seekers trying to say whatever they need to sell a bed.

They sell you unnecessarily expensive stuff

Imagine that you tend to get motion sick and a salesman is standing in front of you trying to sell you a car: "The engine in this car is made from a new metal, it makes the driving smoother and more comfortable, and that effectively prevents motion sickness. Granted, it costs ten times as much as a normal car, but you want a car where you don't get sick, right?"

Would you buy that car? Would you buy it without testing it? Would you buy it without testing it and checking if the salesman was telling the truth about that smooth driving and that it eliminates the risk of motion sickness?

No, I thought so.

Still, that's how the bed business works.[22] The people that own these stores earn big money from people like you, people with back pain and that are desperate for any help. They know that you've heard that sleep is good for the back.

"Maybe it's a better bed that's missing", they tempt you and then add: "Only 3,000 pounds."

By the way, 3,000 pounds is small money in this context.

You could easily pay double that, if you wanted to. Or ten times as much![23] That's a lot of money for a bed like that.

A lot of people fall for that here too. According to a survey by the International Sleep Products Association, 21% of the mattresses sold during 2005 cost more than 1,000 American dollars.

Those twenty-one percent is equal to 1,3 billion dollars! And that number could be too low, according to a furniture magazine.[24]

Since I've been in the business for many years, I know certain things, so I can say that these prices are unnecessarily high.

To begin with, the prices are jacked up a huge amount. As with all branded products, you pay a certain amount of money simply for the brand. There aren't many brands that differentiate from each other enough to make it worth buying one brand above another. But even more importantly: You could easily get a 20-30% discount when you buy a bed. Almost a third of the price is air!

Another important point is that there are no proper surveys done on what type of bed or mattress is the best. The manufacturers and salesmen use statements from happy customers as quickly as they can, but for each happy customer from Tempur, there's also one from Select Comfort and one from Hästens. What you like is so individual that you can't say for sure that one thing suits everyone. Or more specifically: Nothing suits everyone. That's why it's not true that expensive mattresses (or expensive exercise equipment, to mention another business) are better than any others.

The risk of buying a more expensive bed is also more emotional:

---

22 What I write about the bed business from here on is also true for other businesses such as chairs, shoes, exercise equipment and tools. It would just end up going on for ever if included them all here. The point is, that you should think twice before you buy something that costs more than you would pay in a normal store.

23 Hästens model Vividus is often thought of as the world's most expensive bed. It costs 50,000 dollars!

24 https://www.deseretnews.com/article/660201849/50000forgoodsnooze.html

If you worry about whether you could really afford the bed or not, you'll hardly get what the manufacturer promised. On the contrary, the new, ergonomic bed could be a bad idea for your back. The financial stress is not good for your back problems.

And that's how we come to the most important point. This is what you should focus on if you're considering buying an new bed. Are you ready?

Your sleep, and thereby also your back problems depend on many other factors than just a bed or pillow. By focusing your concerns on one specific thing, they've decreased the problem. Expensive beds are another "cure everything"- thing.

In the same way you shouldn't forget the placebo effect. If you buy an expensive bed and expect to sleep well, then chances are that you will. But that doesn't mean that the bed did what it was intended to do. It means you got help to deceive yourself.

What you really need

The opportunities to find shoes that give you the perfect support, a chair where you automatically get the correct posture, a workout ball made from durable materials, a mattress that gives your spine the most support, support for your torso, the right personal trainer and so on are endless. You could spend weeks searching the market.

The big question is really *if* these products or services work. I'm sure some of them work great.

The question is what's most effective. That is, what should you do to focus on the thing that will give you the most pain relief and cure your back problems the quickest? Everything but the thing that does the most is stealing your time. They're stealing time from the thing that could help you.

If you want to spend your time picking out products in a department store or online, then that's your choice, but be aware of what you're doing. To find the right colour on your water bottle, the perfect workout clothes, the complete sweat towel or the Rolls Royce of shower slippers, it may be fun, but it won't make your back any better. You don't need to spend time reading the right exercise magazines or eating the latest diet food either. Instead, you should spend your time, money and energy on the right things.

And that's how we get to the most important question: What do you really need? What's the right thing? Or the opposite, what's unnecessary?

Not only am I going to give you a (somewhat) complete list. I'm even going to give you guidelines for what this will cost. I'll give you a hint now: It won't cost 5,000 pounds.

The first thing you'll need is a *good pair of shoes* – walking shoes or tennis shoes. Make sure that they aren't worn down unevenly or crooked (in case you're using your normal shoes), that the heal has enough soft filling and that the arch of your foot is supported. Other than that, the shoes could look any way. But try to speak to someone who works in the shoe shop to get some proper advice.

Cost: Preferably under 100 pounds. Higher than that, and it's your choice.

Then, you'll need a *mat or a thin mattress* to lie on when you do some exercises. Take a mat or mattress you have at home. It should be softer than a cemented floor, but harder than gelatine sweets. Soft and fluffy sofa cushions aren't very good, since cushions slide around and you need some resistance.

Cost: Starting at 0 pounds.

You also need approximately *2 hours a week* for your exercises.

Cost: Use your regular hourly wage but remember that this is an investment where you can measure the results in your future salaries.

Clothes: Optional.[25] Comfortable and loose. Wear what you have at home.

Cost: Starting from 0 pounds.

TOTAL COST: Approximately 150 pounds

25 At least if you're exercising at home.

So, you don't need: A gym membership, a new bed/mattress and workout ball. You'll be fine as long as you have a bed, some floor- or ground space to lie down on or can go down to the toy store and buy a football for 5 quid. If you don't have that, you've most likely got bigger problems than what you should buy.

One point of view some people have is that the fee for the gym membership makes them fight harder. If that's the case, then it may be a good investment, assuming it's the only investment you're making to find motivation. But don't spend more than a hundred pounds or so on that.

The question is if you're ready to spend 150 quid on your back. There's a chance that you'll change your mind when you realize that this is actual money and investments instead of "impulse shopping" a bed for 5,000 pounds on credit. But, it's time for you to face the music and look at the situation with clear eyes: 150 pounds is less than 5,000 pounds! And when the whole loan is paid off, the bed may have cost close to 7,000 pounds. Is it worth it? You risk feeling more guilt and that causes not only worry but also back pain. So, go cheap and make a smart choice instead of buying something expensive and worrying.

What you can also buy

It sounds a little silly that it would be enough with good shoes, something to lie on and clothes from home, doesn't it? But you don't need to come up with extra things just to have an excuse to go shopping. As the cartoonist Frank McKinney "Kin" Hubbard wrote:

> *"The safe way to double your money is to fold it over once and put it in your pocket."*

That quote won't stop you from going wild with your hard-earned money for some hand rubbing salesman's products. The amount of bed stores, exercise equipment salesmen and health advisors make it very clear. You want to spend money on becoming healthy.

Okay, but if that's the case, you should spend the money on things that will make a difference and refrain from the rest. Put the money in a savings account instead.

The following list are of things that actually work, but that aren't completely necessary:

> *Massage* could give you the relaxation you need to ease the pain for a while. It's not a cure, but according to the world-known professor Kerstin Ulvnäs-Moberg (whom I've mentioned earlier), the massage causes the hormone oxytocin to be released. Oxytocin is among other things known as the "love hormone". The downside of massage is that it becomes expensive long-term or could test your friends' patience when it's not needed.
>
> A lot of people ask me about beds. "Which bed is the best?" "Which bed suits my back?" "Should I lie on a soft or firm bed?" Since I previously sold Tempur beds (I don't anymore), I've seen a lot of happy buyers, but I suspect that the other brands also have happy customers. For more information on what you should think about when you're buying a new bed, check out page 188.
>
> A good *chair* affects you more than you think, especially if you sit down a lot, for example at work. It shouldn't be too soft (since this will cause the muscles to tense to support you), it should have support for your lower back, make sure that your weight is distributed to your bum cheeks instead of the back-side of your thighs, and it should preferably have both foot- and arm rests. Also see if you can lower and raise the chair so that your feet properly reach the floor.[26]
>
> Visiting a *therapist* or a *psychologist* could help you release some of the tension in your back. If you've been in pain for more than six months in spite of doing all the exercises, it's worth looking into this option. See page 73 for more information.
>
> I get questions about *gym memberships* a lot. Which one should you get? Which wellness institution should you go to? Sure, there are personal aspects involved, but a survey by

---

26 Loïc Burn, Michael S. Sinel, William W. Deadorff Treating your back & neck pain for dummies (2007), JohnWiley & Sons, Chapter 14

Svenskt Kvalitetsindex show that people are most happy with Friskis & Svettis. Also, don't only consider the price, but also think about the customer service, the standard of the facility, security and staff competency. Ask people you know of which gym they're most happy with, or search online for phrases such as "great gym" plus your area.

Note that you can't pay to get rid of back pain. Even if you buy the greatest chair in the world, it doesn't matter – if you don't sit properly in it. The perfect shoe is useless as long as it's in your closet. Your behaviour decides whether the money was well-spent or not.

In reality, the best tip is to buy one thing at a time. Don't buy barbells, workout clothes, a bed, a mat, and a bunch of other stuff because you think it might be cheaper or more convenient to get everything at the same time. More than half of it will only be used once or twice. Instead, focus and buy one thing at a time. Let the habit to use that thing (or service) sink in before you try the next thing (or service). Chances are that you'll feel more done with shopping this way. You've saved money, but more importantly: You've shortened the time it will take before you're rid of your pain!

How to make a good deal

If you still want to test one of the things that aren't necessary, but that you feel gives you a sense of luxury in everyday life (and how other people see you?), there's really only one basic rule: It should seem as if you've paid more than you did. An exercise shoe that looks like it costs 300 pounds can be found for half the price or less.

The more bargains you find, the more of them you can afford. You do have to draw the line somewhere though for what is considered reasonable. Otherwise, it's more about shopping than looking after your back. It makes me feel cautious, since it's a sign that you're not ready to do anything about your pain.

It seems like you need a certain knowledge in finding good and cheap things or services. It's very possible that you can find the occasional bargain in other ways that I introduce here, but we're talking about increasing the chances to find those bargains, not individual cases.

Good deals start way before you get to the cash machine to pay. It starts at the planning stage, with the question: "What do I need?". A lot of people step into the trap right away. The majority of people actually buy *what they want*, not *what they need*. In other words, they let their feelings take control over what they buy. It's a very common trap. This is how you get around it:

The answer is never an item or a service. "I need a bed that gives my lower back extra support" is a bad answer. A better answer would be "I need something that helps me sleep better" or "I need something that helps my back to relax". These answers focus on the problem that the item or service could solve, that is the *purpose*. There could be a huge number of items or services that can solve the problem more efficiently than your first thought. That's why it's important to widen your scope and not be single minded.

I've done this mistake a few times myself, I've gotten hung up on one solution, the last time was a few weeks ago when I was going to buy a present for my wife. (It wasn't an anniversary or anything like that, I just happen to like giving her things.) I'd imagined a present of a certain kind and had to go to five different shops before I found something that was even close to what I had in mind. This resulted in me being pretty unhappy once I'd paid for my purchase. When my wife got the present, I had to bite my tongue to not tell her about what she should've really gotten. To her, the difference would've probably been very small, and since she was happy, this "mistake" didn't matter.

Here's the point: If I'd thought about the purpose instead of getting hung up on a certain item before I'd even seen the options, I'd been able to enjoy seeing my wife open the present.

When the purpose is clear to you, it's time to see *yourself* as a part of a pattern. Others have of course had the same purposes as you in the past. That means all kinds of useful research has been done. Use that. There are lots of websites online that compare prices, quality, reviews and much more. There are also places where common questions are answered. On page 203 in part 4, you'll find some tips on how to do good online searches.

When you find a cheap place to shop in, *take out cash* that covers the whole price. Go there fifteen minutes before closing time, suggest a price that's 20-30% under the price tag and reach over the cash at the same time. Don't be too pushy but show that you're a decent person. In more than half the cases, you've now done a better deal than others that buy the same thing. I've tried this from both ways. It works. We're not very used to haggling in Sweden, but in spite of that, it works. The feeling of making such a good deal is also an absolute joy for the love hormones in your body, which means that you're saving money while helping your body to recover faster. Very cool!

Lie 5: "You'll get addicted to back medication"

THE IRRATIONAL FEAR OF PAIN KILLERS

Pain killers aren't anything to fear

During a visit at a friend's medical clinic, Malmö, 2007

Action, you could tell, was his kind of film. Car chases, shooting and probably a Harley Davidson jumping from the roof top of a building to the roof of a bus. In his imagination, he was probably the hero that took a bullet in his shoulder and shook it off with a look that said "that's nothing – you should see the other guy."

He was just the same in his clinic. And he was in pain. You could also tell that he was in pain whenever he tried to bend his back slightly.

I couldn't help but smile in recognition towards my friend as a doctor and got a nod back. His patient was just about to turn down the suggestion of taking pain killers. He wouldn't say it straight out, but you could tell that he thought that pain killers were for women with PMS and kids with ear infections. Together, me and my colleague had seen the same thing so many times.

However, this time we were surprised.

The hero had a completely different thought: "Wouldn't I become addicted?"

As if he'd get a prescription of pain killers and automatically start to get the shakes without his drugs. Maybe, if it had been an American action movie. But in reality? It's not usually that simple.

As long as you follow the recommendations, chances are minimal that you would develop an addiction.

On the other hand, there are good reasons to try pain killers. When you have smaller issues, that most people experience every now and then, pain killers could be the only thing needed to make your back better. And if you're suffering from big problems, pills can give you enough "time off" from the pain so that you can work on the actual job of strengthening your back and healing the injuries.[27]

How you create your own addiction

The chance of developing an addiction to pain killers is minimal, but it's there. It's easy to explain how people most commonly become addicted, but it's not as popular to talk about.

Because the big risk is you and your judgement. Or to put it another way: Your fear of becoming addicted is causing the addiction. If you happened to become addicted that is.

It may seem to go against your gut feeling but stay with me until the end and you'll see why it's not so strange. This is how you face the biggest risk for addiction:

When you're back is hurting and you're about to take a pain killer, you'll hear a voice in your head saying that there's a chance of you becoming addicted. You don't want to be part of that. At the same time, you're hurting and you know that the pain killers will help. So, you're thinking that it might be enough to take one pill instead of two, as prescribed, or only twice a day instead of three. The smaller dosage isn't enough, and when you realize this, you stop taking them all together. You're fine without them anyway. Most days anyway. Some days you take a pill just to get rid of the worst of the pain.

Then some time will pass before the back pain becomes unbearable again. You continue to take the pills you have in the same way. Or you'll go to a different back expert, get a new batch of pain killers and keep taking them occasionally. One prescription follows the next and there's no end in sight. Soon, it'll be even more important to get rid of the pain, and it becomes hard to not take the pills. You've now become addicted.

The description in *American Psychiatric Associations* diagnostic manual is pretty striking:

> *"When an individual persists in use of alcohol or other drugs despite problems related to use of the substance, substance dependence may be diagnosed. Compulsive and repetitive use may result in tolerance to the effect of the*

27 Sarah Key Back sufferer's bible, Random House, 2000, page 169.

drug and withdrawal symptoms when use is reduced or stopped."[28]

As the cherry on top, the pain will never completely go away either.

How you avoid getting addicted to pain killers

Even if the chances of becoming addicted are small, the consequences are not very fun.

You can search online for the signs of substance dependency, but to simplify:

* You're experiencing sweats and difficulties sleeping when you try to quit.
* You're not getting the same effect from the pain killers that you used to.
* You see different doctors for different prescriptions.
* You're trying to get pain killers even though you're not in pain.
* Luckily, it's quite simple to avoid the biggest risks. By using this list, your chances are much better:
* Start with over the counter pain killers, but don't use them longer than a few days. Go and see a back expert instead.
* Inform your doctor about all the medication you're taking. NOTE! This includes herbal medicine, that could really clash with regular medication and that overall pose bigger risks.
* Make sure you get a stop date, and that you're not meant to just take one pill whenever you're in pain. This is especially true for prescription drugs.
* Follow the recommended dosage, but make sure it's as high as possible. Don't take any more. You're not going to develop an addiction, but there's a good reason: it could be poisonous.
* Don't forget that it could take a while (up to several days) before the pills have full effect. The medication is building up

28 https://behavenet.com/substancedependence_

in your body before it reaches full effect.

* Continue to take the entire prescription. Otherwise, the problems may return, the doctor may not be able to determine whether the pills are working or not and you'll receive several prescriptions one after the other. You could possibly decrease the dosage if your doctor agrees to get used to being without them.
* Don't mix different pain killers. It could damage your liver or kidneys seriously!
* Talk to your doctor after the prescription and evaluate how it's worked. If these pills didn't work *for you*, there are a lot of alternatives left.

Don't forget to keep any medication out of reach of children. Even a small amount of aspirin could kill small children!

If you in spite of everything are experiencing extreme problems when you're trying to give up pain killers, there are a lot of places to turn for help. A good start is the NHS website where you can search for support near you in the UK on: https://www.nhs.uk. They have a lot of experience in supporting people like you (and not just homeless junkies, to humour your prejudices).

What kind of pain killers should you be taking?

The pharmaceutical industry is full of different products that may seem a little frightening. There are actually only two different groups of pain killers.

If you're guessing "safe" and "dangerous", I'm giving you detention. No medication sold today have any severe side-effects if you take them according to the recommendations.

No, the two main groups lessen pain in different ways.

One group is called NSAID[29]. But you don't know anyone who says NSAID. It's too difficult to remember. Everyone will instead give you different examples of NSAID medication: Acetylsalicylic acid

29 https://behavenet.com/substancedependence

(also known as *aspirin*), and *ibuprofen*. There are more too. What all of these have in common is that they prevent swelling and help with inflammation. When the swelling and inflammation goes down, the pain will disappear. *Paracetamol* is not anti-inflammatory, but only works for swelling.

To make it even simpler, these pain killers work in the body's nerve endings and stop the pain signals from reaching the spine, where we interpret the signals as pain.

Some kinds of NSAID have been around for a long time. Aspirin (in Sweden known as *Magnecyl* and *Treo*) is for example so old that it's no longer patented.

Normally, pain is a positive thing, since pain prevents the body from being injured. One example is if you're hanging upside-down over a burning hot fire wearing only underwear made from thistles and have bitten down your nails too much.[30] The spine will then send signals to the body to attempt to find a way to put an end to it. When the pain becomes long lasting and is lacking the external causes shown above, the pain transforms from something positive to something negative. Aspirin or ibuprofen will no longer help, and you'll be forced to find something stronger.

Here enters the other group of pain killers. Instead of preventing the pain impulses from reaching the spine, it numbs the spine. The body feels the pain, but can with the help of medication say "So what?"

This kind of alternatives for numbing have been around even longer than aspirin, at least since the 1500s. The downsides of these are also bigger. Mainly, they're much easier to become addicted to.

I'm not going to keep you waiting any longer. The other group of pain killers are based on opiates. The most well-known kind is *morphine*. Another is *codeine*.

All pain killers are meant to be used over a limited amount of time, but it's especially important when it comes to morphine and other opiates. They're strong and it's not good to numb the central nervous system for longer periods. If you haven't improved after the first prescription, you have to make sure that you're not just automatically given the next one.

---

30 It's not a very common example, but school sure would've been more interesting than with the example of a hand on the stove.

But trust me, it isn't in any back expert's best interest to see you develop an addiction to morphine or codeine. That only results in a lot of paperwork. Nah, jokes aside, we have chosen our profession because we want to help people, and making people addicted to strong numbing substances is not part of it.

The pharmaceutical industry is not Satan

You don't have to search very long to find people that dislike the pharmaceutical industry. The industry hasn't done enough to deserve our love:

* Prices are increased regularly even though the pharmaceutical business' have great profits.
* Hard lobbying to approve patent extensions by creating "completely new" medication that are only new in the same way a pancake-recipe is new because you put icing sugar on them.
* A fairly small amount of money is put on development of new medication. Instead, the giants buy up smaller companies that have done the research and reduce their competition at the same time.
* They invite doctors on trips and conferences to get them to prescribe the expensive versions of a medication instead of the cheaper ones.

And so on. One of the world's largest revealer in this field is a Swede named Peter Rost. He's written several books, for example Whistleblower and has a blog where he writes about the same topic: http://www.peterrost.blogspot.com/.

But even Peter Rost is very careful to point out that most people in the pharmaceutical industry are dedicated to the goal of giving you the best possible medication. There are so many checks from when you start working on a medication until it's out on the market that you can be sure that what's on the instructions is what you should be following:

This is how one chemist writes down the rules that each pharmaceutical company must follow:

"Let's say that a company wants to make a new medication. What do they have to do? For starters they have to design scientific tests that prove that the final product is free from contaminations, identifies the ingredients and confirms the amount of medication in each pill. The tests also have to prove that the equipment used to do the testing is clean, that the chemist's preparations are correct and that the equipment performs the same each time. The company also has to develop a method of tracking how the product deteriorates with time. This "stabilization study" must identify and quantify all the new substances that are created when the product ages. (This is also used to show that the levels of the active ingredient don't go below what the label states. If it does, the company could be prosecuted for false marketing.) It must be proven that the products that develop when the medication degrades are safe to consume. Each batch of medication that is shipped out must be tested with these methods. Part of each batch is saved in stock and the purity and safety of these are controlled regularly.

When the manufacturer finally gets to the manufacturing part, they build a factory that meets strict health-, safety- and environmental laws and then they order the raw materials from a distributor. These materials are also tested for purity, identity and freshness. Each part of the equipment at the factory has to be cleaned, inspected and calibrated regularly. While the medication is created, a test is sent to the lab to make sure that everything is going according to plan. The finished product is not allowed to leave the factory before it has been approved by an expert team of professional biologists and chemists. If the nerds reject the product, it often means that the entire batch is destroyed and thousands of dollars are lost. Each step is documented and checked by at least one supervisor.

Data from the chemical tests are usually sent directly to the data systems that then time stamp them and save each separate test so that no bad results can be ignored. The mathematical equations that are built into the system are checked for errors before the manufacturing even starts. In spite of this, the final results are confirmed with manual calculations after each test, just to be sure.

As you may imagine, this manufacturing process creates a huge amount of documentation measuring a few ten centimetres high. Sadly, a group of men and women have the unfortunate assignment to double check everything one last time. Each mistake and minor problem have to be explained in writing by the person who is the reason behind it and corrected according to specific rules to avoid confusion or counterfeit drugs. Larger mistakes or failed tests end with longer and more strenuous investigations that could lead to the process starting over again and all efforts until that point being in vain.

– Matt Fiore, American chemist

I do apologise for the long quote[31], but I want you to understand that the pharmaceutical industry is just as serious as the shipbuilding industry or the airplane building industry. At least the ones that deal with real medication. The ones that deal with quacks, many people that deal with herbal medicine for example and everyone who deals with homeopathy don't have anywhere near this kind of cool and thought through process to manage the questions "what if it doesn't work" and "what if it's dangerous".

31 http://www.randi.org/site/index.php/swiftblog/ 661hidinghomeopathybehindrealscience.html. The process is called Good Manufacturing Practices (GMP). See the website of theWorld Health Organisation: http://www.who.int/medicines/areas/quality_safety/quaity_assurance/production/en/

Who stands to gain from you fearing drugs?

As I've said before, there is no magical wand to wave around to get rid of your back pain. But medication is one of the easiest options for you to find the energy to look after yourself. And as I described above, the process of creating a new medication is meticulously controlled.

Despite the strict rules regulating quality, a lot of people are afraid. Not necessarily for developing a substance dependency, but more generally scared of medication. It's a vague feeling that's almost inexplicable, but it's a fear nonetheless.

The quacks naturally like this feeling since it leads you (and your wallet, don't forget your wallet!) straight into their open arms. They're patiently waiting for you to express that vague feeling of unease about using pharmaceutical medication and they're ready with answers to most of your worst fears.

If you're one of the people who might feel that it's a little cold and inhuman with medication with these eight-letter names, then know that they come from "natural" substances. As if arsenic and horse shit wasn't natural. And as if "unnatural" things like propranolol[32] or Bacillus Calmette-Guérin[33] hasn't saved millions of lives.

If you were to then hint at the side-effects scaring you, then they'd tell you about their miracle medication that not only cures what you're suffering from right now, but also a dozen other troubles. Because if you don't mention any side-effects then there aren't any, right?

"The body manages itself" is a good starting point. But sometimes the body needs a bit of help. Just enough to work things out by itself. Naturally, I'm not referring to the obvious situations where the body can't manage on its own, for example when battling cancer or a severe hernia, where operation may be the only way to save the life or mobility of a person.

---

32 http://www.randi.org/site/index.php/swiftblog/661hidinghomeopathybehindrealscience.html. The process is called Good Manufacturing Practices (GMP). See the website of theWorld Health Organisation: http://www.who.int/medicines/areas/quality_safety/quaity_assurance/production/en/

33 Bacillus CalmetteGuérin is a modified version of the bacteria Mycobacterium bovis, that causes tuberculosis. BCB is the world's most known vaccine.

No more lies

The lie about the pain killers is the last lie I'm mentioning in this book. You've got a pretty good idea of how bad it can get when you see a back expert. You know what to look for and what's really going on with these things.

But you don't even know half of what you should know to get proper help from your back expert. We still have a lot to go through.

From here on, you'll find out some truths about the back experts and your back. Some of the truths could very well shock you.

Inconvenient Back Challenge Nr. 6

Before we get to the truths, it's time to remove yet another boulder from the backpack that's slowly been getting lighter. This is a boulder that approximately 120 billion people around the world share, and as a back pain patient you're at even greater risk. This is about recovering from depression. You can feel down every now and then without it meaning anything, but if you're feeling down for over 2 weeks in a row, then it may be time for you to do something about your depression, because that's what it is.

There are a lot of ways to manage depression. For example, I'd like to start by encouraging you to get help, even if it may be something you don't really have the energy to deal with. There are a lot of different treatments that work, including medication.

But you can do a lot of things yourself. In actual fact, this is where the challenge starts: choose one of the following six activities and do it every day for one week. When it's been one week, add one more activity, until you're doing all six of them. Continue to do them and connect them to a trigger (see page 81) so that they become part of your everyday life.

* Go outside. To see the sun for 30 minutes helps your body stabilize your inner clock, which means that you'll sleep better.
* Get your pulse up. When you move properly for half an hour or so, the body releases endorphins that decrease stress.
* Consume Omega-3-fats. You get it from fish, spirulina or tablets. It's been proven to be anti-depressive.
* Sleep. Have a set sleeping schedule. Read more on page 177.
* Spend time with people face to face. You don't need to talk about the serious stuff. Have fun. Keep it simple by for example going to see a movie.
* Stop brooding. As soon as you realize that you're thinking about something negative, stop yourself. Don't forget the 21 days without complaining on page 61.

There are a lot of people you can phone, for example the National Counselling Society (01903 200666) or find the closest therapist or counsellor near you in the UK on https://www.nhs.uk.

PART 3: THE INCONVEINENT TRUTH

"The most essential gift for a good writer is a built-in, shockproof shit detector."

– *Ernest Hemingway, American author, in an interview with Paris Review 1958*

A hobby, a glass of red wine and get laid

Far from the space where the patients are, back experts are balancing on the line of the rules of confidentiality. Not that they're gossiping, but back experts are people too and they have needs to talk about things they've been through. Wouldn't it be interesting to listen in on one of those conversations?

One thing that back experts keep coming back to, almost like a standing joke, is the phrase "a hobby, a glass of red wine and get laid".

- The same patient is back again, one back expert sighs.

- Twentieth time? The other one asks.

- Thirty-second. He carries around a lot of concerns.

- Ah, he's missing a hobby, a glass of red wine and needs to get laid.

It may sound a little harsh to wave off someone's pain and concern with these kinds of recommendations. That's why no back expert would ever say that to a patient.

But there's a lot of truth in the things that back experts would never say. Many patients would get a better life if back experts could or dared to recommend what they were thinking. Those kinds of truths are quite common among back experts – but you censor yourself.

In this case, it's pretty obvious that it would actually have been good to recommend their patients to get a hobby, to drink a glass of red wine or to get laid. Let me explain:

When you're working on *a hobby,* you're not only focused on what you're doing, but you also forget the pain. There are two even bigger reasons to get a hobby:

* You're having fun, and that causes the brain to release endorphins which make the body heal faster and make you feel better.
* You have a greater chance to meet other people, which usually

leads to you moving more. When you move more your back becomes stronger. A stronger back prevents a lot of problems.

Put aside a little time to do the things you really want to do, even if you're not sure if your back can handle it. Rake leaves, collect stamps or play poker with the guys. Go to a sauna. Sing.

Red wine and other alcoholic drinks is a very multifaceted topic. That's why it's important to be careful with your choice of words here:

* Do we have to have a bad conscience? Most adults drink alcohol. Is it that bad? Alcohol in small amounts spread out over a week rather than getting drunk every Saturday (and maybe on Wednesdays too) isn't a bad thing. Alternate a glass of wine with a glass of water throughout the evening.
* How much am I allowed to drink? Men shouldn't drink more than 14 standard glasses per week. Women shouldn't drink more than 9 per week. A standard glass is 15 cl wine, 33 cl beer or 4 cl schnapps. The more you spread it out across the week, the better.
* * Is alcohol good for you or bad? Both. It depends on how much you drink. A little can help prevent diabetes, but a lot can be the cause of it. A small intake could also protect against heart- and cardiovascular diseases, but a high consumption during a longer period could give you high blood lipids and a high blood pressure. The liver gets the worst of it. It can't keep up if you drink too much. There are more risks[34]
* Are you having drinking problems? Here's a check list. You may have problems if you...

  - use alcohol to escape from issues and concerns.
  - use alcohol to help you sleep.
  - drink every day.

34 https://www.nhs.uk/livewell/alcoholsupport/therisksofdrinkingtoomuch/

- are starting to feel that alcohol is one of the most important things in life.
- drink alone regularly.
- have friends that recommend that you drink less.
- become irritated when people criticise your drinking.
- are feeling guilty for your drinking.
- need a glass in the morning to cope with the world.
- feel shaky the morning after you've been drinking heavily.
- can't remember certain periods of time when you were drinking.
- are having problems at work due to drinking.

* What do I do if I'm having problems? Find help. Alcoholism is difficult to manage alone. You could for example phone Alcoholics Anonymous on their helpline on 0800 917 650 or Drinkaware on 0300 123 1110 in the UK. These are the two main organisations, but you can also find help at your local GP and at rehab centres. On the NHS website you can search for the closest support facilities: https://www.nhs.uk.

In other words, drink a glass or two to de-stress but not to become drunk. Alternate with your hobby and you'll get even better results.

Lastly, to get laid, means to have some good sex, and I'm serious about this one. You feel a lot better when you're having sex. Besides the tension before and the short euphoria feeling has a lot of nice benefits...

* Your relationship with your partner gets better.
* The love hormone oxytocin spreads in your body and reduces your chances for cancer (including prostate cancer) and heart diseases.
* Your body becomes relaxed and less stressed.
* Women get fewer menstrual cramps.

* You get better protection against colds.
* It reduces the risk for migraine in some people.
* It's a good way to exercise because it strengthens your muscles in back, bum and stomach as well as your heart.[35]

Sex comes with so many positive effects for the body that it's hard to believe. Some people say that it's up towards 60 positive effects.[36]

That it feels good is of course also a benefit.

It's not only because of physical reasons that you should try to get it on: Sex is very much a social activity. For most men it causes a higher confidence, and for women it could be an outlet for their feminine side.[37]

The more intensive sex, the better. And you don't even need to have a long-term relationship or be straight: Find someone, use protection and go for it. Or "take care of yourself" if you're experiencing a dry spell, even if it doesn't quite have the same effect.

***

Collectively these three shocking advice are said with good intentions and are all about relaxing and enjoying life. But you understand why it can't be said so bluntly.

---

35 More information on the expert site About.com: http://stress.about.com/od/generaltechniques/a/sexandstress.htm and http://sexuality.about.com/od(sexualhealthqanda/f/orgasms_health.htm

36 The website AustralianWomen's Health lists 56 positive effects for both men and women that are supported by science: http://aulifestyle. yahoo.com/womenshealth/ article//5934418/56reasonstohavesex/ The magazine Forbes doesn't count, but they write "sex is necessary" and it should be both regular and enthusiastic: http://www.forbes.com/2003/10/08/cz_af_1008health.html.

37 The website Healthmed writes in an article "Sexuality: Use it or lose it" that women who don't have sex regularly run the risk of losing the ability to enjoy sex: http://healthmad.com/menshealth/sexualityuseitorloseit/

Truth 1: Think in opposites!

HOW YOU'RE BECOMING MORE "ANTI"

"Contradiction is not a sign of falsity, nor the lack of contradiction a sign of truth."

– Blaise Pascal (1623-1662), French mathematician, philosopher and physicist

Since the mid-1900s more people have learned to help themselves, to not "take any shit" and to do things that feel right. There are lots of books that break away from old-fashioned conceptions of satisfying other people's needs and thinking about yourself first.

In most cases this is a positive development. People need to be more selfish and focus on what they want. At least in contrast to what every other person is doing. By definition, you can't become any better than the average if you follow the pattern. Considering how the average person is doing, that thought is pretty depressing. Think about how small the odds are for you to become rich: It'll take you an eternity if you save money, to win the lottery you need to be incredibly lucky[38], and getting your hands on an inheritage isn't as easy as it used to be.

Don't let your feelings control you

"The happiness of your life depends upon the quality of your thoughts.

– Marcus Aurelius (121-180), Roman emperor

In one regard, it's not as good to dwell on your thoughts and feelings, and that it when you're sick or are suffering from an ailment such as back pain.

The reason is that your brain is deceiving you when you're feeling

38 The chance of winning the National Lottery in the UK is approximately 1 in 14 million.

a bit under the weather.

Or to say it in a different way: Your brain doesn't always know what's best for you, since it's not ready for modern society. It's trying to solve problems in the wrong order and it struggles with solving several problems at the same time. Especially when the problems are physical and partly psychological or emotional.

That's when one of those ”good news/bad news”- situations arise. Let's deal with the positives first.

The good news is that you can help yourself along the way by doing the opposite of what you think you should be doing. Think backwards or in opposites of what you're feeling when you're experiencing problems and you'll solve a lot of your problems.

Instead of thinking ”no”, think ”yes”. Instead of thinking ”it's never going to work”, think ”I can do this”. Instead of ”there's never anything good on TV”, think ”I'm going out for a bit”.

We're going to look at exactly how that works now. First, some negativity, so that the book won't be criticised for being too optimistic.

The bad news is that you've already done what you think you should've done. You've gone after what other people say or write or followed your gut instinct. If you're going to learn how to think in opposites, you have to first de-program yourself and get back to the starting point. That can be difficult. But don't despair. You're not alone, and more often than not you just need a little more information and a nudge in the right direction.

Let's get started!

Remember, it's never the right time

”Life is not measured by the number of breaths we take, but by the moments that take our breath away.”

– UNKNOWN, POSSIBLY ERICA FRANDSEN, GEORGE CARLIN OR AN ANONYMOUS POET FOR THE CARLETON CARDS.

There is no right time, no ideal opportunities to exercise, stop smoking, go on a diet or learn something complicated. Waiting for the right time is something your gut feeling uses as a trick to keep you stuck in your bad habits a little longer. That's why you sometimes have to go against that and "just do it". Enjoy your bravery instead.

And when it comes to back pain, one of the biggest challenges is to continue on as usual, to move, work and to be social. You can be like you usually are even if you don't believe it.

A big advantage in continuing with your regular life is that your body is used to it. Another is that you don't have to put in so much effort to find your way back to your normal life afterwards.

Spend time with people, even if you don't want to

"Nothing is impossible for the man who doesn't have to do it himself."

– *Earl Wilson (1907-1987), American journalist*

Staying in contact with friends and family is extra important when you are in pain. If you're on sick-leave, they become your main connection to the normal world. Otherwise, they can be your biggest cheerleaders when everything's hard and the visits to the back expert are anything but tempting.

I'm too aware of how little you want to socialise when your back is hurting. You just want to be alone. To be able to get stuck, be alone and not think about anyone else. And preferably feel a little sorry for yourself too.

It can also be difficult to socialise and play nice when you're in a bad mood all the time. Comments come out sounding harsher than they meant to. The world feels a little more hostile.

But people can handle that you're a little grumpier! And it's not so bad to just go along with things when other people are talking. Chances are that it goes a little like when you're having sex: A little hesitant at first, but after a few times you'll realise that it's pretty sweet to have people around you.

It is, if nothing else, a good way to remind yourself that the world keeps spinning even though you're going through something. Your friends go on – some get promotions at work, others take holidays and some of them are going through the same problems they've had since you got to know them.

A few things to think about when it comes to friends:

1. There's a limit for how much they're willing to listen to regarding your back pain.

It's enough to mention that you are in pain. People get tired of the rest of it after a week or so. I'm sure you have other sides to you that you'd like to showcase. If you still need to get it off your chest – contact a support group. Ask your back expert or search for some online.

2. Be cautious of the sympathy and the attention you're getting.

Most ailments bring with them two kinds of benefits, or as we call it: "primary and secondary sick gain". The primary one is about how easy it is to use the ailment to your advantage (get out of doing the dishes for example), especially if people are starting to thread carefully around you.

The secondary gain is regarding how other people give you help and sympathy (boxes of chocolate and flowers are some of the typical signs). Both of these gains will make you less inclined to want to get better. Who wants to lose access to free sympathy? You! You want to. Because that sympathy will go away soon and turn into creeping suspicions of you going along for a free ride.

Another big benefit about spending time with people while you're suffering from back pain is that it takes a lot less time to recover and catch up. You don't miss as much when you don't isolate yourself: The wonderful comments of your friends' children, good films, rude people on the street and so on.

Be generous, even if you don't want to

"You can't help everyone said the cheap person – who didn't help anyone."

– *Marie von Ebner-Eschenbach (1830-1916), Austrian author*

People who are ill or have big problems, almost always turn into egotists. It's a survival strategy, but that strategy came about around the time people lived in small tribes in Africa. We've evolved a lot since then: Among other things, we've become social. The group is so important that it's hard to tell which is more important today: Ourselves or our group of people.

When we're not feeling well, it's extra important that we're not just focusing on ourselves. Research has proven that one of the best things you can do to feel good is to make someone else happy, basically to be generous.[39]

Generous people live longer, make more friends and are in average happier than other people. To help others is also something that gives a kick that "lasts" longer than any other kind of joy.[40] That kick will among other things help you to endure your back pain, while at the same time making someone else happy. It's a "win-win" situation, as they say.

A few suggestions on what you could do:

* Ask some family members that live far away to stay with you for a few days.
* Invite your friends over for dinner.
* Buy something nice for your partner.
* Donate money to research.

---

39 Elizabeth Dunn, Lara B. Aknin, Michael I. Norton "Spending Money on Others Promotes Happiness" University of British Columbia, Science, 2008, quoted in RichardWiseman 59 seconds, Chapter "Happiness".

40 Martin Seligman is a psychologist who researches "positive psychology". Check out his TEDtalk (Technology, Entertainment, Design): http://www.ted.com/talks/martin_seligman_on_the_state_of_psychology.html

* Buy the magazine that the homeless people are selling (come on, you can afford it!).

Do things that hurt

No one likes being in pain, but if you don't have another choice, you have to learn how to live with it and do things anyway.

In actual fact, it's better than you think for you to do things that hurt. To for example lift things *wrong* gives your back exercise. When you take a walk, even though your back hurts, you're showing your back who's in charge and are at the same time improving your muscle strength. As long as the pain isn't unbearable, you can use it to map out *who you are*, that is, where your limitations are. And finally, the pain is in many cases in your head, not your back. You're afraid of the pain, and that makes you smaller than you are.

Personally, I'm not religious, but a poem by Marianne Williamson reminds me that I shouldn't allow fear to rule me:

> *"Our deepest fear is not that we are inadequate. Our deepest fear is that we are powerful beyond measure.*
>
> *It is our light, not our darkness that most frighten us. We ask ourselves, who am I to be brilliant, gorgeous, talented, fabulous? Actually, who are you not to be?*
>
> *You are a child of God. You playing small does not serve the world. There is nothing enlightened about shrinking so that other people won't feel insecure around you.*
>
> *We are all meant to shine, as children do. We were born to make manifest the glory of God that it within us. It's not just in some of us; it's in everyone. And as we let our own light shine, we unconsciously give other people permission to do the same.*

As we are liberated from our own fear, our presence automatically liberates others."

- Marianne Williamson (1952-), American author

The fact that you are in pain is not the end of the world. It doesn't mean that your life is over, it just means that it's something you have to learn to live with, the same way you may not have perfect eyesight or feet the same size.

You may even learn how to use the pain. Pain (the whip) does not work as well as a carrot for motivation, but you take what you have, as Kajsa Ward said.

This is how it works:

1. If you can, choose the option that hurts the least.
2. Sometimes it doesn't matter what you choose. Everything hurts. If that's the case, then choose the option where you will move more or where you'll get other physical benefits.
3. Try to get into a work flow, so that you can forget the pain temporarily. The flow usually comes when you're doing something that you're interested in and that includes repetitions so that you can disconnect your brain to a certain extent and just be in the moment.

Create more problems

"There is nothing so wretched or foolish as to anticipate misfortunes. What madness it is in your expecting evil before it arrives!"

– Sir Winston Churchill (1874-1965), British prime minister and Nobel prize winner in literature

No problem is as big as the ones we're currently experiencing. The problems we're currently having tend to be the greatest we've *ever* encountered. The thing is just that we're solving problems all the time too. But we don't think about that as much.

If you look back on difficult problems that you've previously had to deal with, I'm sure you struggle to understand why they were so difficult. It's because you solved them, moved on and see things differently now.

You can do this with your current back problems too. I understand that your back problems may not be solved as easily as your previous problems, but you don't actually have to solve the problems before you move on.

Think in opposites. Create new problems.

Most of us try to avoid problems: We're afraid of conflicts and we try to do the right things from fear of uncomfortable consequences. But the conflicts and consequences that emerge from the new problems are often much easier to solve than your back problems.

By creating new problems above and beyond the problems you're already experiencing, you'll notice that the old problems aren't as important anymore. They just seem small in comparison. But that requires new problems that consume all your attention. Don't try to create artificial problems but think about what your real challenges in life really are. Chances are that you're facing bigger challenges than your back pain. Start working on those problems. Are you unhappy about your work? Are you having family issues? Is your home falling apart? What charities are you passionate about?

Inconvenient Back Challenge Nr. 7

You only have 6 boulders left from the original 12. It's time to stop being a workaholic. You often hear that being a workaholic is described in a positive manner to show that a person is dedicated and makes things happen. In actual fact, it's often the other way around: Workaholics often lave things unfinished.[41] Besides, you risk wearing yourself out and become a stranger to your family. If you've got time off and are spending the majority of the time thinking about work, you're most likely a workaholic. If that's the case, it's now time to take on this challenge. During 30 days:

* Set up limitations for work. Go home when the work day is finished! No exceptions. Everything else can wait for the next day. Start finishing things twenty minutes before it's time to go home.
* Get a new perspective by taking breaks. You'll work more efficiently and you won't have to work as hard.
* Write down your ideas when you think of them, instead of trying to make them happen right away. Most of them won't seem important a few days from now.
* Spend time in nature. Reserve half an hour in your calendar every day for nature experiences.
* Stop neglecting your friends and family. They're at least as important as your work. Do a 80/20 analysis to confirm that, see page 30 for more information.
* Find a hobby that is unrelated to work. What have you always wanted to do?

41 Se till exempel de fyra typerna av arbetsnarkomaner på: http://www.webmd.com/balance/guide/workaholism

Truth 2: You don't need an operation for your hernia

To be operated on with a hammer

Everyone who has a hernia, and some other people ask when they can have an operation. Some of them demand to be operated on "NOOOW!", without anaesthetics if need be.

Actually, there's nothing that says that you have to have surgery, and there are a lot of reasons to think more than once about whether you really want to go through an operation.

When you're in pain, and hernias hurt – you just want everything to be fixed. *Now!* But I'd like to warn you from agreeing to an operation before having all the facts. If you still decide that you want to have the surgery, and your back expert agrees, then at least you know what to expect.

Why do people want surgery?

As the American psychologist Abraham Maslow wrote:

> *"I suppose it is tempting, if the only tool you have is a hammer, to treat everything as if were a nail."*

Most patients don't have a lot of education in how you determine if someone should have surgery or not. They think it's the only solution. Surgery becomes their only "tool".

In most cases, back experts are nice guys that give their patients alternatives, but more back experts than you'd think only give one recommendation and expects the patient to just say "yes, please". Preferably without thinking about what other options there might be. "If that's what the back expert said, then that's how it is."

Remember, it's always you who have the last say in the decision making, and the back expert can't do anything against your will, and you're the one who cares most about your body.

This means that you could end up in a situation where you're going against the back expert's recommendation and that's scary. The back expert probably isn't thrilled either. But brace yourself. You've got all the right in the world to make sure that everything works out the best way it can in the end. (Often, as I said at the beginning of the book, you're not in the kind of hurry that you might think.)

Other back experts are bad at explaining why surgery isn't the best option and come off as if they're only trying to advise the patient against something that would remove their back pain forever. That isn't the case. Back experts have many more tools available, and they may know facts that make surgery unnecessary or even harmful.

It's trickier when the problem lies with you. You may think it's such a good thing that ”something” is happening, that you don't care what it is. Especially if you've been waiting for a while and the pain isn't giving in. In these situations, most people make an unfair comparison between ”doing something” and ”not doing something”. In actual fact, you are doing something. You're finding out more information. That's better than jumping in head first into something that may make things worse. If you haven't done your research, you won't know if you're going to be in worse shape after it's over.

What is a hernia?

A hernia is in general when a part of your body is leaking out in a different part of your body, or through a natural opening. Now over to the back.

The spine consists of muscle, bone marrow, nerves and two things that people usually think about when talking about the back: plates and discs. The plates are pieces of bone that are between 1 and 6 centimetres high. Between them you have the discs. They look like rings, are hard as car tires on the outside and soft as tooth paste on the inside. This works well, since the discs are the shock-absorbers of the plates.

Unfortunately, the discs can break or change shape, either by leaking out the internal contents or so that the disc is protruding. In both cases, this puts pressure on nerve endings and that hurts.

Most commonly, a hernia is caused when the level of water in a disc has gone down enough for the disc to crack. The discs get drier as you age. That doesn't mean that all old people have hernias. Actually, hernias are most common among 40-year olds.

Another, smaller cause, is that the plates are pressed together or turned too quickly or too much. But according to research, people with heavy manual work don't have any more worn out discs than people in general.

Even if a leaking disc sounds serious, it's not enough to hurt. The nerve root also has to be inflamed. We think. Because no one knows for sure why people get hernias.

Do you need surgery?

There isn't any one, simple answer when it comes to hernia surgery. I'm not going to tell you what to do. But I can give you some points of view that you could think about:

1. Get help from a back expert – if he or she *doesn't see any other option*, and other independent back experts agree, then surely there isn't any reason to hesitate.

2. Most hernias heal on their own. The pain disappears after a few months, even without surgery, with the help of rest, medication, injections and rehabilitation. You have about a 50% chance to recover within a month. After six months you have approximately a 90% chance to be more or less symptom free. That means, there's only a 10% chance that you need to have surgery.

3. If you're experiencing an incredible pain, numbness or weakness in your bum cheeks and down your legs, this is called Sciatica and is caused by a hernia, then surgery may ease your pain. You should be considering surgery if you've had severe Sciatica pain for more than four weeks. An operation cures leg pain easier than it does back pain.

4. If you're experiencing moderate to severe pain, you're most likely going to experience a quicker ease if you have surgery.

Pain that interferes with your everyday life and demands huge amounts of pain killers are often helped through surgery. But 5-10 years after the operation, your daily life will be the same whether you go through with the surgery or not.

5. The back expert will do a manual examination and do an MRI and/or tomography and/or myelography to find out if you need to have surgery. You need to be in enough pain and have a hernia that is operable for the back expert to feel that it's worth it.

6. There's always some risk when you go through surgery. Chances are often small, but you could get bleedings, infections or back injuries. Furthermore, there are risks with the anaesthetics, even for healthy people.

A clear list for your decision making can be found in part 4 on page 234.

If you do decide to have surgery, it's good if you prepare yourself for having to exercise to recover quicker. Rehabilitation and things like that. It will take time. Again, there is no easy way out.

WARNING! If you're experiencing difficulties urinating and have reduced sensation in your genital regions, you're most likely suffering from the cauda equina syndrome. If that's the case, it's very important that you have surgery as quickly as possible (within eight hours) to avoid any permanent issues!

Truth 3: The back expert does not want your life story

HOW YOU CAN ESTABLISH A GOOD RELATIONSHIP WITH YOUR BACK EXPERT

As a patient, you often feel close to your back expert. This is especially true when it comes to someone you have physical contact with, such as a physiotherapist or someone who does a thorough examination by hand. The back expert is also in superior position with their knowledge and power. This often stirs some feelings in people.

But I assure you, that feeling is one-sided. Not only do the medical ethics prevent all romantic relationships and friendships. It's not even enough that the short amount of time keeps the back expert from having time to get into feelings and thoughts about mutual interests. No, it goes a lot deeper than that. You take on a professional role where the patient is transformed from a person to a patient.

Anyone who's tried acupuncture, massage or any other treatment where you're wearing very little and are in physical contact with your back expert should be happy about this. Because, it means you have no reason to feel embarrassed for having bellybutton lint, warts on your feet or hair on your back. Instead, you'll be seen for the things that matter, the reason you're there. What else could you want?

If you're thinking about whether any erotic feelings are involved or not between a back expert/massage therapist and patient, know that if so, they are *initiated by the patient*. There may however be exceptions among the quacks, since no one is regulating them. It's likely that the majority of everyone who's been in contact with patients within healthcare for a longer period of time, have at some point been misunderstood when they're trying to help a patient. I was once offered approximately 800 pounds by busty woman in her 50s to escort her to dinner in London. I've also received several shameful suggestions both from men and women during my time as a massage therapist, but as all professionals in the field, I've politely declined and then neutralised the tense situation with humour.

But there are other aspects in this truth too, back experts don't want to know everything about you. When you understand these aspects, you will find it easier to get the help you really deserve.

How the first meeting takes place

The first meeting between you and your back expert is important because you will go through a lot of things, often during a short amount of time. It's easy to get overwhelmed or stressed, and especially to feel down when things don't go as planned.

The first appointment is your best chance to set the right tone for your relationship. Think about this as if you were interviewing your back expert for the job. You can't hire all the applicants, so you have to choose the one who is most suitable for the job.

To get this right, it's helpful to know what's meant to happen during your first meeting. This is how an average first-time appointment looks:

* A short introduction
* "So why are you here today?" – A short description of your problems and symptoms
* A review of the relevant facts of your medical history, for example chronic diseases, operations and organ dysfunction
* Your social relationships
* "Are you taking any medication?"
* "Do you have any allergies?"
* "Do you have any questions?"

The back expert's last question, whether you have any questions or not is a tricky one. A lot of patients are confused and worried or come up with irrelevant questions that they immediately regret. Of course, you have questions – you just can't think of them right this moment. Now you know that you'll most likely be asked that question, so you're prepared. On page 227 there are lots of questions for you to choose from.

Don't try to be a hero: It's *okay* to bring this book with you to the clinic, or a note where you've written down the questions you'd like answered.

The difficult first question

I also want to take this chance to warn you about the first question: "Why are you here today?". It's not as easy to answer as you might think.

Back experts and especially doctors have a lot to do and think about. Their schedule is tight, each appointment consists of questions and manual examinations. As if that wasn't enough, the next patient is sitting outside the door waiting for their turn. A pile of papers are lying in the room next door, waiting to be dealt with so that the next meeting won't start over from the beginning again.

In most cases, a back expert will only have time to listen for a few minutes to what you have to say about how you're feeling and why you're there. Out of those minutes, the first 10-15 seconds are the most important. The back expert has heard enough stories to be able to categorize you into one out of maybe 5 or 10 ailments based on one or two symptoms. The rest of the time is spent trying to confirm the suspicion or find alternative explanations.

Imagine what happens if you say the wrong things during the first 15 seconds. The back expert will come to the wrong conclusion and everything you say will be interpreted based on that. I once said the wrong thing in the beginning, and it only end up with a battle of "no, that's not what I meant". I once had to tell the person in front of me to forget everything I'd said and start over from the beginning since he was trying to push an ailment onto me that I knew I didn't have – just because I named the symptoms in the wrong order.

There isn't enough time to put a lot of focus on your thoughts and feelings about the different symptoms, your theories about what happened or details such as where an accident took place or who was present at the time. Your life story isn't interesting, no matter if you've won an Oscar eight times or have two Porches in your garage. You should be happy about that. That shows that the back expert is focused on the right thing – fixing your back.

Back experts like things to move quickly

You've got two options when the meeting is coming to an end. I'd like you to think about which alternative you think we like the most:

1. You finish on time, thank him or her for their time, set up a new appointment, end with a smile and do right by paying when you leave.
2. You hang around even after your appointment has come to an end, ask more questions and tell him or her about new problems, start talking about what you're going to do this weekend, have fourteen difficult layers of clothing to put on, say ”bye” five times before you actually leave and end up staying another five minutes while you're finding out if you really have to pay.

Before you arrive, it might be a good idea to think about *who* you're going to see. Is it your best friend or your back expert? It might seem insensitive to come down on those who act like option 2, but it isn't meek and overly polite people I'm targeting, but people who lack respect for others.

Even if you mean well and you're being polite, time flies. If your appointment is running this late, it will affect the next patient, and even the one after that. Imagine you're the next patient – would you like the patient before you to act like that? That's why you should be as efficient as you can when it's time to leave. It will pay off, because it's easier for us to be polite next time we see you.

Inconvenient Back Challenge Nr. 8

The myth that asking for help is a sign of weakness is so strong that a lot of people believe that successful people never ask for help. That reasoning could lead to you walking around too long with back pain or continue to go to a bad back expert which might make your injury worse. That boulder has to go.

First of all: No one who is successful is afraid to ask for help. It's important to know your strengths and weaknesses, and to delegate so that other people can feel like a part of the process. You don't seem dumb either: You show that you're willing to improve.

During these upcoming 30 days, practice asking for help by contacting someone face to face and...

* Tell them what you know about the problem. Show them that you understand how it usually is and what you're struggling with.
* Then, bring up what you would like to accomplish (not what the person should do), and ask for feedback or thoughts. Suggest an option ("Should I...") rather than asking an open question ("What should I...").
* Ask for tools to understand the situation if you can't suggest an alternative option. For example: Ask if there are similar situations or if other people have had the same problem.

Don't go to the obvious people but ask your contact's contacts too. Who do your friends usually ask about these problems?[42]

---

42 Three people who have written about this are Howard: http://blogs.hbr.org/cs/2009/11/asking_for_help_the_smart_way.html, New York Times: http://www.nytimes.com/2007/07/07/business/07shortcuts.html and Dr Deb: http://drdeborahserani.blogspot.com/2008/08/howtoaskforhelp.html

Truth 4: Your back will improve if you stop abusing drugs

HOW YOU GIVE UP THE "JAVA JIVE"

For most people, it's obvious that drugs are bad. You destroy your body. But the difference between what's classified as drugs can be a bit unclear. To be very clear: There are many substances that aren't as dangerous as heroin, but that are very addictive. They're also harmful to your body – and to your back.

It's extremely tiresome to lecture and forbid things, so I'm not going to do that. As long as people follow the laws, they're entitled to do whatever they want. But I'm still going to give you my professional opinion. I share this opinion with thousands of other back experts, doctors, health experts and scientists. The point is, it's a lot smarter to live a healthy life style. Not just in general, but it is actually better for your back if you drop some of your bad consumption habits. At least trim them down.

If you don't enjoy these kinds of lectures, I recommend that you read more about the Darwin Awards. It's a prize for a very special kind of prize winner. As they write on the official website:

> *"Named in honour of Charles Darwin, the father of evolution, the Darwin Awards commemorate those who improve our gene pool by removing themselves from it."*[43]

The point is that people are sometimes too dumb for their own good and more often than not it ends the way you said all along. The odds are not in your favour if you're using any of the following drugs.

Reduce your coffee intake

You won't like this. If there's one thing you're not allowed to say in

---

43 The text is taken from: http://www.darwinawards.com/

Sweden, it's anything that would threaten the coffee break. I know bosses who have managed to change work tasks, move around who's in charge of who and even meddled with the holidays without problems, but have turned the entire staff against him- or herself by suggesting changes to the coffee breaks. You don't touch the coffee.

That's why I'm going to start off with some good news.

The effects of coffee are still unclear. New investigations are constantly made, but so far it doesn't seem harmful to drink a few cups of coffee a day.[44] Some research even hints at some caffeine being good for the body. Not as good as moving or sleeping well, but still alright.

This is where the bad news start: If you drink more than two-four cups of coffee or tea a day, the risks increase quite quickly. This is mainly about the symptoms you see in people with back pain: Stress, depression, difficulties sleeping and personality changes (mostly towards increased grumpiness).

Since caffeine gives you a feeling of alertness (it stimulates the central nervous system), it's best to watch out. I know how tempting it can be to jack yourself up on coffee. There was a time when I was basically living off of coffee. For many people who are feeling tired, it's often easier to put on a pot of coffee to get a momentary fix than to take a break or a proper snack so that the blood sugar levels slowly rise to normal. If you do this a few times, it's not a big deal. But if you live of caffeine, wake up because of it and feel bad if you haven't gotten your daily dose of caffeine, then it might be time to think about whether life should be that way or not. Chances are high that your sleep cycle and metabolism will be disturbed and that the body is put in a constant state of ready to go. These things almost always give people back pain.

Don't try to go cold turkey. It's doomed to fail. Instead, do what hospitals do when they give massive doses of opium or morphine to burn victims: Gradually decrease the dosage from a full dose to your recommended daily intake. From five-sex cups to four and a half. Pour the last bit out into the sink. Then four cups. And finally, three cups.

---

44 Mer information på Medline Plus, som är webbplatsen för amerikanska nationalbiblioteket för medicin och hälsoinstitutet: http://www.nlm.nih.gov/medlineplus/caffeine.html

Coffee isn't that good after all, not really. Not good enough to have back pain for at least.

If you do drink coffee, don't be cheap and buy the cheapest kind. Chances are that the cheaper coffee contains higher levels of harmful substances. You're worth high-quality coffee.

Give up smoking

I'd think that you need your lungs, windpipe, mouth and sinuses just as much as everyone else. If that's the case, smoking isn't a great idea.

But enough about cancer.[45] This book is about back pain. It turns out that cigarettes and tobacco are generally bad for your back. Tobacco not only:

* worsens your stamina, which makes it more difficult to move – that in turn worsens back pain.
* decreases the blood circulation, which slows down removal of waste products and makes the supply of new oxygen less efficient.
* makes you grumpier, which decreases your chances of recovery.

No, there's one reason to quit smoking to get rid of your back pain: Tobacco makes it more difficult for the body to heal. It means that you could shorten your recovery time by giving up smoking. You can't claim that you're doing everything you can to get rid of your back pain if you're insisting on smoking.

Research about smoking shows so overwhelmingly clear how harmful it is, that it's hard to understand that people are still doing it. You can't claim that it makes you cool, when you're having chemo treatments.

Just like with coffee, the trick is to slowly reduce the number of

45 Exactly how much bigger your chances for cancer are has been calculated by the American Center for Disease Control:
http://www.cdc.gov/tobacco/data_statistics/fact_sheets/health_effects/effects_cig_smoking/index.htm

cigarettes you smoke. Don't try to be a hero and give it up cold turkey because your body has become properly addicted to the nicotine. Instead, start by counting how many cigarettes you smoke each day, and prepare a visible count down calendar where you reduce the amount step by step, so that you see how many cigarettes you have left on a specific date. Set a date approximately two months away, so that you give yourself a good chance to succeed. Then reduce the cigarettes one at a time. Set up a good reward for yourself once you've made it and celebrate.

If you're having problems quitting, join a group. It will be hell, but it's easier to deal with it together. That means you can also make sure succeeding is something prestigious.

Anyway, if my father who has been smoking for over 40 years can quit, so can you. He had tried everything, all the courses and treatments, but hadn't managed to break the habit. Smart as he is, he thought of *using* his own behaviour. Like most men over 50, he's a cheap skate (even if I'd never tell him). By calculating how much money he spent on cigarettes every month, he could split this into the days of the month. He started to put that exact amount of money in a jar every day and started to see how the money grew. That made him quit once and for all, something that really impressed me.

If you've planned to try this method, it's important that you put money in the jar every day. Seeing the money grow is what will keep you motivated. This is how it can look: A cigarette pack costs about 10 pounds. With four packs a week, that would add up to 40 pounds. In one year, that adds up to 52 weeks times 40 pounds = **2,080 pounds**. If you're two people smoking in the family, you could afford a Thailand trip for you and your kids, every year. Those dreams don't have to be dreams any more.

Eat to live, not to clear the plate

Being overweight makes it more difficult to recover from back pain. Not everyone is overweight though. Here's how you find out if you need to lose weight:

* You have a *Body Mass Index* that measures over 25[46]
* Most of your fat is around your belly.
* You have high blood pressure, diabetes or high cholesterol.
* You've gained more than 10 kilos as an adult.
* You exercise less than 30 minutes a day.

If you answered yes to several of these questions, you're at risk for secondary diseases, as well as a longer recovery period for your back pain. Go to a doctor and ask for help. Above everything else, eat less. Your body doesn't respond well to overeating. Your back doesn't like the extra weight since it has to carry it around day and night.

But you know this. If you are like most westerners, you've tried to do something about this with diets.

So many people are stressed because they know that they should lose weight, and this has become a problem in itself. Or two problems in fact:

1. They're feeling so stressed about losing weight that it's not fun. Instead of biting their tongue and saying no to everything that is tastier than its energy value or a specific requirement, the focus should be on the goal. And the goal is to find a fun enough way to reach the goal to make it worth the effort.

2. They cheat, find excuses and defend behaviour that they know is wrong. The damage is double now, since they feel that they can't trust themselves any longer. These things have a way of spreading to other aspects of your life. To be perfectly clear, losing weight creates more liars than any fishing around the world or bragging about penis size *and* everyone who claims that they win while playing poker online put together.

In the end, the entire weight matter has become a big tangle of abuse. Wherever you turn, there's something to get you high: Sugar highs,

46 BMI is calculated by taking your weight in kg, for example 75 kg and dividing it with your length in meters times itself, for example 1,70 x 1,70 = 2,89, which put together gives you a BMI value of 24,4.

the warnings, the warnings about the warnings, the lies you tell and so on.

The solution is in the motivation. Have you thought about *why* you want to lose weight? If you're going to succeed, you have to first find the motivation to do so, and it can't be that you "know that you should" or because "it's good for you". You have to find something that makes you excited, hopeful and motivated. When you've found something specific, you can let it take up your mind in a positive way. That way the temptation of crisps or ice-cream won't be as strong, and everything that promotes the goal will become all the more fun. I know that this is hard, that's why you'll find extra help towards the end of this chapter.

Stress less

No one can avoid stress completely. Missed buses, accidents, financial problems and so on almost always come with a faster heartbeat, adrenalin rushes and fight-or-flight reactions. That's normal. But to live with constant stress and pressure isn't good for anyone. [47]

Neither is it good for you, I might add, since you most likely see yourself as an exception to the rule. Or someone who's not affected by these things. If that's the case, you're abusing stress.

It's even more dangerous to try to hide or push away the stress. But everyone who are more than mildly stressed more than once a day, or very stressed more often than once or twice a month should re-think this.

Your back does not respond well to stress. There's a lot of research about this, but one of the people that has written the best about the topic is Dr John Sarno at the *New York University Medical Center*. Sarno has, as I mentioned before, written the successful book *Healing Back Pain*. In the book he writes among other things about how people with a strong driving force to "succeed" and a big sense of responsibility, a lot of discipline and perfectionism, have a higher

---

47 Some people, for example Timothy Ferris in a 4hour week, differentiate between good and bad stress. Bad stress (dictating bosses for example) makes you weak and lowers your selfconfidence. Good stress pressures you further than you thought was possible and gives you higher selfconfidence.

risk for stress-related back pain.[48]

When you're facing a difficult situation, you may think that you'll calm down after a minute or so. Instead, your thoughts shift over from your conscious to your subconscious. There, they transform to instructions that are sent to the muscles to tense or even cramp. Since the brain thinks that the problem is the physical pain, that's where the body spends energy instead of dealing with difficult situation itself.

The solution for stress-related back pain is that you first need to be aware of it and understand the causes behind it. After that, you can feel the emotions. Only after that can you learn how to deal with the emotional stress and get a life that contains less stress.

You don't need expensive therapy or talk about whether your parents appreciated you. That rarely leads anywhere. What you can do, is to have a few proper talks with someone you feel comfortable with: A friend, a parent or a colleague. Try to work out the problem once and for all. Bring paper and a pen so that you can write down your conclusions, so that you won't need to invent the wheel again next time you're experiencing the same feelings.

For a lot of people, stress often leads to anger. It can be tempting to let the anger out by cussing, shouting, punching things or by acting poorly. But research shows that by venting your anger, it actually grows stronger.[49]

However, there is one effective method: Sit still for two minutes in quiet room. If the reason for the stress is minor, you can distract yourself by watching a fun film, going to a party or doing other things that could lead to lower stress. [50]

Is the stress major, then there is a technique that is proven to

48 Some people, for example Timothy Ferris in a 4hour week, differentiate between good and bad stress. Bad stress (dictating bosses for example) makes you weak and lowers your selfconfidence. Good stress pressures you further than you thought was possible and gives you higher selfconfidence.

49 B.J. Bushman "Does venting anger feed or extinguish the flame? Catharsis, rumination, distraction, anger, and agressive responding", i Personality and Social Psychology Bulletin nr 28, citerad i Richard Wiseman *59 seconds*, MacMillan, 2009, kapitlet "Stress".

50 B.J. Bushman "Does venting anger feed or extinguish the flame? Catharsis, rumination, distraction, anger and aggressive responding", in Personality and Social Psychology Bulletin Nr. 28, quoted in Richard Wiseman 59 seconds, MacMillian, 2009, Chapter "Stress".

work: Spend a few minutes describing the *benefits* with whatever is stressing you out. You could for example feel stressed because you don't have a lot of money, maybe you've learned to live on the cheap or discovered some kind of entertainment thanks to this situation. To just spend a few minutes on "benefit-thinking" is often enough to give a big effect on how you think about the triggering stress factor later on.

If all of these techniques fail, try going on a holiday. You need it. I can still see myself on that holiday where I sat shouting at the internet café, because I was that stressed. I also remember the revelation of me and my wife not doing any of the things I'd longed for and planned to do during the holidays: Eat long breakfasts in bed and take nice, long walks. You could also do what I did, extend the holidays in case you feel that you haven't had enough rest. All potential obstacles (that your boss wouldn't approve, that you can't afford it, that you're not worth and so on) are just excuses. You have to see through the excuses and make the decision you know is right.

If I, with my 70-hour weeks, and my three businesses, could take two extra weeks then you can definitely do what you need to find your way back to yourself. A few days or so might be enough. Because it's only when you take the time off that you get away from the stress.

With so many types of drugs (*and* depression, Law of Jante, sex, alcohol...), I hope that you manage to minimise your worst bad habits. Like the 80/20 principle says: It's enough to remove the biggest 20 percent of the reasons for you to avoid approximately 80 percent of the problems. So, what is your drug of choice, and what can you do? Whatever it is, it will affect your back pain more than you think.

Inconvenient Back Challenge Nr. 9

You require self-control to succeed with losing weight. We've already removed that boulder from your backpack, so go back to page 38 and repeat if you've forgotten what we said.

A lot of people also give up on their diets because they consume too few calories and feel tired. If you for example follow a low-carb diet (remove potato, rice, grain, pasta and bread) and substitute rice for spinach, you should remember that half a cup of rice is the equivalent of 300 calories, while the same amount of spinach only contains 15 calories. That's why you need to add leguminous plants such as beans, peas, lentils and soybeans.

There are other things you can do too, that most of the people who have lost weight usually do. First of all, they ignore all the advanced recipes, since those are next to impossible to follow because something is always missing. Instead, find somewhere between 3 to 5 dishes with healthy raw products for lunch, and the same for breakfast and dinner and all the other meals. Keep it simple. Rotate between the dishes every day, whether you're home or out. To eat the same thing again and again (that is to make a habit of eating that specific food), makes a huge difference.

The other thing you can do to lose weight is to stop consuming calories in soft drinks, milk and juice. Drink water instead (a lot of it!), unsweetened tea or coffee without milk or cream, or wine.

The third action you can take to lose weight is to take one day off every week! Make Saturdays your "eat-whatever-you-want"days: Eat sweets, drink coke, buy ice-cream and crisps. Go overboard, so that you almost feel sick thinking about sweets during the rest of the week. Paradoxically enough, these feats help you lose weight since they make sure your body isn't slowing down the metabolism, so enjoy eating some junk.

Give this method a month. All you have to lose is a few extra kilos. Somewhere between 5 and 10 of them.

Truth 5: Lumbago is a hoax

WHAT DO YOU DO WHEN YOU HAVE A "GENERAL PROBLEM"?

"Lumbago" – from the Latin 'lumbus' ('hip, loin'). "Weakness in loins and lower back"

A lot of people that see a doctor with severe back pain is referred to a physiotherapist with the diagnosis "lumbago". We can see a clear problem with getting a diagnosis here – it's nice to be able to tell your friends and family something, but the diagnosis should mean something too. What does lumbago mean?

In English you usually translate lumbago to "lower back pain". The problem is that lumbago and lower back pain are two big umbrella terms. It's as if your car's dash board said "General problem" instead of all the different lights such as "go and get petrol", "check your oil", "put on your seatbelt" and "close the door".

What do you do when you have a general problem?

A website writes the following about lumbago:

> *"Lumbago is an umbrella term for lower back pain, which can be caused by a variety of issues from sudden strain to tumours."*[51] *(italics added by me.)*

You'd think that you need a few different types of treatments for strains and tumours, and you do. That's why the term lumbago gives patients some comfort, but not much help in finding the right treatment.

Even *Encyclopaedia Britannica* are critical:

> *"Lumbago is considered by health professionals to be an antiquated term that designates nothing more than lower back pain caused by any of a number of underlying conditions."*

---

51 S.E. Smith "What is lumbago?", http://www.wisegeek.com/whatislumbago.htm

Why do back experts use the diagnosis Lumbago?

There are two main reasons for why doctors still give you the diagnosis of lumbago (it's mainly doctors –physiotherapists, naprapaths, chiropractors and orthopaedists know better than that):

1. You get rid of the patient

Most patient problems do not require the back expert to do anything since the back will heal itself after some time. With a general diagnosis that does not require special treatment other than the usual (short rest, some pain killers to get started and then exercise and a more ergonomic way of living), the back expert doesn't have to spend time on a patient that shouldn't be there. Instead, he or she can spend the time on the patients that really need the help.

2. A thorough examination has not been done

I guess that some doctors that read this headline take it as an accusation that they're not doing their job. That may be so, but even Dr Bernt Ersson's textbook for future doctors say:

(It's a long quote, but there's a point – I promise.)

"The judgement; "in lack of objective signs of sickness" is often, if coined by doctors, based on an incomplete status, surely correct according to the traditional norms of doctors' education, but compared to the physiotherapist's or occupational therapist's status, this seems lacking, especially regarding the structures related to mobility.

Doctors often examine reflexes, sensibility, muscle weakness and Laségue[52]*, that is excludes hernia or root blockade. Hopefully a traditional general status with*

52 "Laségue" is a test that doctors perform in case a patient has a hernia. The patient lies on his back and gets help to stretch one leg at a time towards the ceiling without bending the knee.

rectal- and mammae examination[53] *will be included as well as normal blood tests. After 4-8 weeks, a plain x-ray will be done of the lower back, often without finding anything pathologically relevant to the pain. Degenerated discs and other "age related" x-ray findings often don't mean anything in this context.*

Sometimes the doctor has pounded the lower back or pinched the patient in various places and possibly even found some sore areas and call this "lumbago" (back pain), "lumbago-Sciatica" (back pain that radiates down the leg) or weak back.

During the above described routine examination, accepted not only in Sweden, of the lower back, it is understandable that "nothing objective" can be found, since the mobility structure has not been examined!

So, a correct but unfortunately lacking status regarding problems related to the back mobility. During what other sicknesses is it accepted that the sick organ is not examined?"[54]

The risk of the Lumbago diagnosis

While the diagnosis lumbago is a comfort for the person who doesn't know what the problem is, another problem pops up, namely what happens now. It's not possible to give any practical tips if the diagnosis is too vague ("general problem"). There's a risk that the patient may take the lumbago diagnosis as a way for the doctor to say "I can't do anything about your pain". Or "I can only give you general advice".

In many cases, that may be so. Ersson continues:

"The truth about lower back pain" is well-known and it's not very flattering for medical science:

53 An examination of the rectum and chest in search of tumours or other changes.
54 Bernt Ersson Grundläggande ortopedisk medicin – Ländrygg, bäcken, höft, Sollentuna OrionFarmos, 1997, page 11

You go to the doctor when you need sick-leave from work or pills, you go to the back cracker to get better!

It's well-known among the general public that doctors have little knowledge about backs! [55]

When will us doctors realise and admit this embarrassing fact?

Of course, patients will understand that doctors don't know enough. Why would they otherwise come to me and other back experts in groups to find out about other possible perspectives of the problem?

I meet a lot of patients that are unhappy with what their doctor has to say about their back pain. Often, I don't need to do very much for them to improve:

* Make sure that the patient stands, sits, lies and moves more ergonomically.
* Examine where the problem is located.
* Motivate the patient to move instead of remaining stationary.
* Give tips of exercises that are aimed for the right area.

It doesn't have to be more difficult than that.

What do you do if you're diagnosed with lumbago?

To be diagnosed with lumbago isn't a huge issue if you compare it with many other things in life. You're not really being fooled, and in most cases it's okay, because the back pain will disappear on its own anyway.

It's mainly if you suspect that something more serious than normal back pain is going on that you need a more precise diagnosis than lumbago or lower back pain.

55 Bernt Ersson Grundläggande ortopedisk medicin – Ländrygg, bäcken, höft, Sollentuna OrionFarmos, 1997, page 12

Sjukvårdsrådgivningen give the following reasons to move on:

* You've had back pain before and this pain is different from that.
* You're getting other symptoms that you don't recognise.
* You don't improve after two or three weeks.
* You have (or have had) brittle bones, Bechterew's disease or cancer.
* And you're experiencing problems controlling your urination and defecation or you can't empty your bowels at all, in which case you need to look for treatment immediately with the GP or emergency room!

"To move on" doesn't necessarily mean to continue searching for a new back expert. More often, it means that you should continue asking around. "Okay, but what is the cause for my back pain/ lumbago?" The diagnosis can be a way to try to make things easier for you, even if it hasn't worked. So, give your back expert another chance.

No more truths

After a few tough truths about thinking backwards if you're not thinking in opposites, hernia surgery, how back experts work, drugs and lumbago, it's time for you to get a crash course in how you get the best treatment. I've collected the best advice so that you can continue on as soon as you've finished the book.

Part 4 is also the big reason why you should bring *Back Secrets* with you wherever you go. There are lots of tips if you see a back expert, but part 4 also includes tips on how you can deal with the social insurance system, your insurance company, how to exercise, how to sleep and so on and so on.

So, what are you waiting for? Keep reading.

Inconvenient Back Challenge Nr. 10

It may be a painful insight, but some people eat up your energy, energy that you need to recover – and you need to get rid of those energy thieves.

By barging into your life, making hens out of feathers, continuously complaining and criticising and never respecting a no, they can become the death of any conversation. If you have these kinds of people in your life, you'll recognise them quickly: You'll feel exhausted after seeing them. These kinds of boulders can't stay in your backpack.

But, it's become a habit to have them in your life. That's why it may be a challenge to stop seeing them. Do this:

* Start a new activity that reduces the time you have together.
* Set up limitations at the beginning of the conversation. For example, "I've only got ten minutes to talk."
* Let them know if a topic is making you uncomfortable. Refer to the challenge of giving up complaining (page 61) and ask if you can compete together.
* Be honest with your needs. Tell them if you need to do something else.
* DON'T try to solve the problems of the energy thief! That's a bottomless hole. Don't even acknowledge the problems.
* Limit eye contact, all sounds that show that you're listening and keep body contact to a minimum.

Think about the energy thief in terms of "life is too short" and say no politely but firmly whenever they come up with new suggestions. It may be difficult in the beginning, but you'll feel happy every time you succeed.

PART 4: A SHORTCUT TO EFFICIENT BACK TREATMENT

"What gets us into trouble is not what we don't know. It's what we know for sure that just aint so."

- *Mark Twain (1835-1910), American author and journalist*

Why are smart people so dumb when it comes to back pain?

Something that surprises me time and time again, and that can really piss me off is how normally intelligent, well-adjusted individuals can be so absolutely stupid when it comes to pain and health. Especially back pain, that is both paralysing and difficult to define at the same time.

They don't ask for help, maybe because of some misdirected image of being "squeamish". If they do go to a back expert, he or she won't listen to the advice in spite of the back expert being well-educated and has helped hundreds of other patients. In fact, they seem to be doing the opposite instead.

To help patients like this isn't easy, I'll tell you that. But with *Back Secrets* in your hand, you'll have so much help that you can't avoid being inspired and go and see a back expert and make sure you get the help you deserve.

Meeting Greta

My clinic, 2004

"Why didn't you come in earlier?" I asked Greta who was sitting in front of me.

"What do you mean?" she asked. My own back almost hurt looking at how hunched over she was sitting.

"When you first came here, you told me that you'd been seeing that physiotherapist for two years. You'd gotten exercises that hadn't worked but you didn't tell him about that. I thought that was all. But last time you told me that you'd seen your GP for back pain a few years ago. She gave you some pills. That didn't help either.

"So?" Greta said and I could see that she didn't see the point I was trying to make. She flinched from pain as she lifted her arm to scratch her head and then tried to hide it from me, her back expert.

"And this time you're telling me that you've been in pain more or less for twenty years. Sometimes it's so bad that you can't lift a milk carton. Once a year or so you're bedridden so your husband has to look after you.”

”It comes and goes,” she said apologising.

I put my hand on my forehead. ”But, please, why haven’t you been looking after yourself? Why have you continued to go to see the same physiotherapist and your regular doctor when it’s obviously not been working? Why haven’t you looked for other options?”

She shrugged. ”Well, it didn’t feel right to just quit. You can’t just abandon them like that.”

”But you didn’t get any better. Greta, you’ve been walking around with your back pain as long as I’ve had a beard. That’s roughly 20 years we’re talking about.

”Yes…”, she said hesitatingly. ”But you never know if anyone else could’ve fixed it either.”

”I can almost guarantee that you won’t find out as long as you’re not trying any other methods, isn’t that right?”

She looked at me with her brown eyes and I could almost see a light coming on above her head. She’s gone her whole life without trying very many new things. It’s probably been safest that way. But it’s also that way of living that has eventually brought her to me.

***

Greta is about 65 years old now, so you might dismiss her as an old loopy lady, but you can’t imagine how many loopy people I meet that are neither 65 years of age or women. Different versions of Greta turn up in my clinic and with other back experts every day of the week. They continue with bad treatments no matter how much pain they’re in. You’d think that they’d see reason after some time, but they don’t.

Maybe they’re unaware of the other options available. If that’s the case, I have a big tip:

If you can spend time on choosing a new electricity company, or which supermarket to shop in, then you can also choose a back expert. Many times, that’s actually even easier.

Get rid of your back pain

UMBRELLA SHOPPING AND LISTS OF COUNTRIES YOU SHOULDN'T VISIT

More than 80% of all people experience back pain some time. There's no guarantee that it won't happen to you. At least not without risking prosecution for false marketing. But, with one simple method you can decrease the risk significantly *and* shorten the time to become free from pain.

That is prevention!

I'm sure you've heard it before, but it's cheaper to buy an umbrella when it's sunny than when it's raining. Umbrellas tend to be lying at home when you need them, but we're talking about something you've always got with you, that is your body. So, spend some time looking after it *before* you need it.

I don't want to come across too much as ”your body is your temple”, but there is some truth in that thought.

Things that cause back pain

Wouldn't it be easy if there was some sort of list of things that cause back pain, so that you could avoid them?

A little like lists of countries you shouldn't visit because there's always a war going on.

There are lists like that. Here's one of those lists of the most common causes for back pain. If you can or can't avoid these things, that's another thing entirely:

1. Weak back muscles

Your suffering from a compressed back or bias. Your back- and torso muscles have become weak because you're lazy or because you've got a job that's more important than your back. Like being an astronaut or something.

2. Muscle- or ligament injuries

One of the absolutely most common reasons for lower back pain. Muscle strains are really difficult and are the reasons for many visits to the emergency room every year. The underlying problem is that the muscle is overworked or strained. The ligaments, that hold the joints together could have been overstretched or become injured in other ways.

3. Bad posture

Your back has taken a beating from all the times you've spent hunched over by your computer (like a banana!), been sitting in deep sofas or been sitting in the car – yes, sitting. You may walk funny too.

4. Stress

You've pulled your shoulders up and tensed your back and neck to the point where the blood is having problems getting through to your back since you haven't learned to prioritise right. This is what happens when you can't think clearly, don't know how to prioritise and therefore spend more time stressing. In the end, you'll be addicted to the feeling of stress. You'll be a stress junkie.

5. Too little/bad sleep

Your back won't have enough time to recover and stretch since you go to sleep at 02:00 AM. Of course, you have to get your daily 5 hours of TV! But then you'll be lying in bed thinking about what you have to do at work tomorrow.

6. Addiction

Your back is forced to carry a lot of extra weight while it's exhausted since you over-consume food, sugar, alcohol, cigarettes and so on. In the end, it's about you not bothering to take care about yourself or because you've given up.

7. Unresolved feelings

Your back ends up being the meeting point for all the feelings that have remained unexpressed since you're walking around tense, trying to not be as emotional as everyone else. You want to be perfect. How's that working out for you?

8. Spondylolysis or spondylolisthesis

Spondylolysis means that a small fracture occurs in the small bows that stick out from your plates. This is most commonly occurring in your lower back plates. Spondylolisthesis is the movement of the plate as a consequence of the spondylolysis. You're often born with this, but it can also occur later in life as a consequence of a fracture in a part of your skeleton.

9. Hernia

When a disc (the flat discs between your plates) cracks, a tooth paste looking content will leak out. If it causes pressure on the bone marrow and nerves, it can result in pain. A lot of people think that they have to have surgery when they have a hernia, but that's not a given at all (see page 133).

10. Lower back pain

Lower back pain is an umbrella term for pain in the lower part of your back that is lacking a specific reason. It's very rarely caused by any specific serious injury or disease.

11. Sciatica

Sciatica pain (pain that radiates down into your legs and feet along the path of the sciatic nerve) sometimes occurs at the same time as your back pain. This could for example be due to a hernia.

If you want to continue further down the list of things that can cause back pain, here are some other causes: muscle stiffness, spinal stenosis, whip-lash, circulation problems, hip arthritis, infections, prostatitis, hormonal changes, anaemia, myopathy caused by drug usage, drug addiction, poisoning, deficiencies, Bechterew's disease, infectious sacroiliitis, Reiter's syndrome, polymyositis, myositis, post-polio syndrome, muscular dystrophy, fibromyalgia, polymyalgia rheumatica, rheumatic arthritis, tumours, soft tissue tumours, osteoporosis, pregnancy, hypermobility, instability, blockages, coccyx pain, rectal ligament pain and trapped nerves. Among other things. You might understand now why it's so difficult to make a simple and specific diagnosis.

Did you notice that you can solve many of these problems with the same kind of behaviour for the rest of your life?[56] If that's the case, good. But the important question isn't whether you know what to do, but if you're actually going to do it. Are you doing what you should be doing? Or is that for everyone else?

The faster you learn that you're included in the odds, the faster you can focus on things that actually work.

4 lethal excuses

Before you can start making things better, you have to stop making things worse in real 80/20 life style spirit.

There are two reasons for why you should stop with bad things. The first one is obvious: You'll eliminate the biggest problems. The second one is that you'll have more time for good things.

In other words, *stop lying to yourself*! You're the only one who will be fooled and you're the one it will backfire on.

You mainly come up with three excuses that make it more difficult to reach good results. All of them are just excuses.

Excuse 1: You don't have time

If you claim that you don't have time to do what you know you should be doing, then you're only fooling yourself. Of course, you have time! You're awake approximately 900 minutes every day, but you're saying you can't put 15 of those

56 Exercise somewhat regularly, eat healthy, sleep properly, do what you can to stay healthy, spend time with your friends and phone your parents occasionally.

minutes on something that will make the pain stop?! You're not that busy. Choose to do this and you'll find enough time. You choose what's important in your life.

Besides, if you don't choose what's important in your life, then someone else will. They'll use the fact that you don't have a plan to help them solve their problems. Without your own plan you'll never succeed in finishing things that are important to you. Choose this now and you'll find time because you'll have taken back control over your time.

Excuse 2: You don't have money

"If I only had 10.000 pounds, I could've done this." "When I have a million, I'll make my dreams come true". To say these things are only excuses so that you can stay in your comfortable zone without having to take any chances. You're blaming the money, when in reality you're the one who needs to change.

Think about it: What does it really cost to make your dreams come true? Count. If you prioritise a little wiser, it most likely won't be an issue, but you may have to pass on that flat screen TV when you get back money on taxes or stop going to the pub and wasting hundreds of pounds because you're buying rounds for everyone. Neither holiday dreams or visions of how you could be free from your back pain are so expensive that you can't scrape together money for it. You can, if you choose to prioritise that!

Excuse 3: You're not motivated

Most people have started projects such as quitting smoking or going on a diet and given up after a week or so. Every time you fail, your self-esteem sinks and with that your chances to succeed next time. We're going to take care of that if you let me.

First you have to understand why you've failed. This is the big secret of staying motivated. The secret is that you haven't fully understood *why* you should succeed. Your motivation hasn't hit home yet and you're not feeling the drive. You may get the idea of losing weight one day and start then. Your motivation at this stage is what we call jävlaranamma in Sweden, this is a kind of primal force of getting things done *now*. With this approach, I promise that you're going to fail. Because you'll run out of juice after two-three weeks – anyone would! No one can keep going only with a primal force of will longer than that. And all attempts to try to change your way of living requires at least six months of work. Because that's how long it takes to create a habit, since you have to re-program a lot of connections in your brain.

Most people in today's society want things quickly, preferably with minimal effort and without giving anything up. The reason for this is that some things that are easy to come by can make us happy for a moment. As Micael Dahlén writes in the bestseller *Nextopia*:

> *"In the Expectation society there are plenty of opportunities for people to be happy. In actual fact, it's never been easier to experience happiness. At the same time, it's never been this difficult to maintain it."*[57]

When it becomes too easy to reach small goals, people won't learn how to plan to fulfil bigger goals, and that's why they never learn how bloody important motivation is. Do you know?

Excuse 4: It seems dangerous

Fear can be useful. It's fear that tells us to leave a burning house. Fear only becomes an issue when it tells us to do nothing.

Fear is one of the most common reasons for why we limit ourselves. Most of us "postpone" (hopefully forever...) things that are hard and live with them for a long time instead of finishing them off right away: You've hated your job for a long time – change jobs, you and your partner are fighting all

57 Micael Dahlén Nextopia: Livet, lyckan och pengarna, Volante (2008), page 19

the time nowadays – find help or walk separate ways, you're facing financial problems – phone a financial counsellor or bank, you've got family issues – find a mediator.

Start checking things off. Or as Steve Jobs, one of Apple's founders wrote:

"About a year ago I was diagnosed with cancer. I had a scan at 7:30 in the morning, and it clearly showed a tumour on my pancreas. [...] The doctors told me that this was almost certainly a type of cancer that is incurable, and that I should expect to live no longer than three to six months. My doctor advised me to go home and get my affairs in order, which is doctor's code for prepare to die. It means to try to tell your kids everything you thought you'd have the next 10 years to tell them in just a few months. It means to make sure everything is buttoned up so that it will be as easy as possible for your family. It means to say your goodbyes.

I lived with that diagnosis all day. Later that evening I had a biopsy, where they stuck an endoscope down my throat, through my stomach and into my intestines, put a needle into my pancreas and got a few cells from the tumour. I was sedated, but my wife, who was there, told me that when they viewed the cells under a microscope the doctors started crying because it turned out to be a very rare form of pancreatic cancer that is curable with surgery. I had surgery and I'm fine now.

This was the closest I've been to facing death, and I hope it's the closest I get for a few more decades. Having lived through it, I can now say this to you with a bit more certainty than when death was a useful but purely intellectual concept:

No one wants to die. Even people who want to go to heaven don't want to die to get there. And yet death is the destination we all share. No one has ever escaped it. And that is as it should be, because death is very likely the single best invention of life. It is life's change agent. It clears out the old to make way for the new. Right now, the new is you, but someday not too long from now, you will gradually become the old and be cleared away. Sorry to be so dramatic, but it's quite true.

Your time is limited, so don't waste it living someone else's life. Don't be trapped by dogma – which is living with the results of other people's thinking. Don't let the noise of others' opinions drown out your own inner voice. And most important, have the courage to follow your heart and intuition. They somehow already know what you truly want to become. Everything else is secondary.[58]

In summary: It's okay to be scared, but don't postpone things you're scared of doing just so that you can be afraid longer. Get help and work it out.

How you sleep better

"A good fit of laughter and a good long sleep are the best cures."

IRISH PROVERB

Exercise is only one of the things you can do to lessen your back pain. Another important thing is to sleep. Yep! I know that it doesn't sound as flashy as lifting weights in front of people admiring you and wondering which sex you're interested in, but sleep and rest are at least as important. While you're sleeping, your back is recovering. For example, you regain one to two centimetres height during the night.[59]

Without a sufficient amount of sleep, you're not able to think clearly and you also become more sensitive to pain and other

58 From a speech by Steve Jobs: http://www.mindpowerindia.com/freearticlesall/01successsecretsandmotivationfromstevejobs.htm
59 This entire chapter owes a debt to the book Good night: The sleep doctor's 4week program to better sleep and better health, Penguin Books, 2006, chapters 12, by Michael Breus.

unpleasantries, such as rude people or failures.

I'm guessing that you're not sleeping nearly as much and as well as you'd like. You rarely sleep 8 hours in a row, as if it was cool to be awake the longest or get up first. Or you're struggling to wake up when the alarm goes off, end up snoozing and still have to stagger out of bed like a zombie.

Do you yawn more than twice in a day? Do you nap during the day? Then chances are that you're not sleeping enough.

The first problem usually is falling asleep. To solve this, I recommend that you keep an eye on when your sleep trains leave the station. *Sleep trains* are the times during the evening when you're feeling extra tired. If you don't go to sleep, then this tiredness will pass and you'll feel alright again, but an hour or so later it will come back. Every evening has a certain amount of sleep trains departing, usually around the same times, and you have around five-ten minutes to go to bed, or you'll miss the train. By keeping an eye on the sleep trains, you'll be able to fall asleep faster.

The room should be dark, fairly cool (approximately 18 degrees) and not have too many things in it.

Why aren't you sleeping?

If you wake up during the night, it's time to find out what's keeping you from a good night's sleep. Chances are pretty big that it's one of the following causes:

1. Stress or worry

When you can't turn off your brain and the high tempo from your waking hours, it's hard to sleep. Up to 75% of everyone dealing with sleeping difficulties suffer from stress or worry.

How you solve this type of sleeplessness:

* Get rid of the TV and computer in your bedroom. The bedroom should be a calm place.
* Breathe deeply – start by breathing out fully. Then fill your lungs so that your stomach protrudes. Breathe out slowly.
* Put a notebook and a pen by your bed. In case you think of something you need to do: Write it down and tell yourself to deal with it *when you wake up*.

* Count down from 300 to 0 but remove 3 each time. That is 297, 294, 291... You can't think about two complicated things at once. Choose this problem, which is limited enough for you to solve before you fall asleep.
* Exercise lightly before you go to bed.
* Have a bath or get a massage from your partner to let go of any tension.
* Read something that won't make you think too deeply – fiction or comics. Definitely no work-related texts.

2. Caffeine

Caffeine can be found in anything from coffee to fizzy drinks, but also in some pain killers, sweets and ice-cream. Caffeine in itself is not healthy, but a more important concern is addiction. I never thought that I was addicted. Still, I failed time and time again to decrease my coffee intake from 10 cups to 5 per day, even though I had a bet with a friend that would come to my house and clean for a full month. I know how difficult it is to break the habit. If you can't hold off on coffee for two days, even though you've tried, find an expert. They've come very far in researching how you treat addiction.

How you solve this kind of sleeplessness:

* Experiment a little, how far before bedtime can you drink coffee, or what can you drink? The effect on you is very individual. For example, I never dink coffee after 14:00.
* Stop drinking coffee gradually.
* Drink a lot of water, and you'll be able to deal with the abstinence problems easier.
* Don't get point cards at cafés and other coffee places, so you won't buy coffee there as often.

3. Others that sleep in or near your bed

Both children that wake up in the middle of the night and a

partner that snores or moves around a lot are common reasons for why people sleep poorly. In average, a person changes position between 40 and 60 times per night. That means that you move around approximately every 10 minutes. That's more annoying than you'd think.

How you solve this kind of sleeplessness:

* If you're two parents, take a shift each. For example, share the night so that one of you take the shift until 2:00 AM and the other takes the shift after that. Use earplugs during your time off at night.
* Make sure that the kids go to bed at a set time so that you get to sleep too.
* Bring in a mattress that the kids can sleep on in case they walk into the bedroom at night.
* Make sure you don't get too much light. Dark curtains are a must. Use a mask so that you won't be bothered if your partner reads in bed or to shut out lights from other lamps.
* Put pillows between yourself and your partner and you'll be less disturbed by his or her movements.
* If your partner is snoring, use earplugs or soothing sounds, for example white noise, rain or water. There are CDs you can buy, but you can also set the radio between two channels to get some white noise – it may seem strange but it drowns out the sounds of snoring.
* Snoring can be helped with decongestant medication or allergy medication, special tape that opens up the nostrils, decreased alcohol consumption and losing weight. Find out if anything in the bedroom could be causing allergies. Avoid medication that relaxes the muscles.
* Use different mattresses since you're both probably of different sizes and prefer different firmness.
* Brush your teeth and try to make sure that no other strong scents are bothering you.
* Avoid pets in bed if not everyone finds it okay.

4. Aches, for example back pain

If your back is hurting to the extent where you can't sleep, it's easy to give up and try to make up for the sleep during the day. This is a mistake! Your inner clock will get confused. You sleep best during the night, in one long session, without waking up.

How you solve this kind of sleeplessness:

* Don't spend too much time in bed during the day or night and day might blend together.
* Lie on your side with a pillow between your knees or lie on your back with your legs on a pillow. In both of these positions your spine will be the least strained. Avoid lying on your stomach or having a pillow by your genitals to keep your spine straight.
* Get out of bed by lying on your side by the edge of the bed and pushing yourself up with one arm while swinging your legs over the edge. Lie down by doing the same thing backwards.
* Try to move as softly as you can.

Nothing serious will happen in the short-term if you can't sleep – the body takes care of this by making you extra tired a little later but do what you can to help your body.

If you're experiencing major problems, then find a sleep expert so that you can get to the root of the problem and find a better solution than I can present here.

How you find good equipment

As I described in the section where they were trying to rip you off because they know you're desperate (Lie 4: It costs 5,000 pounds to get better), it's not that simple to buy the right equipment.

Here is some more guidance for buying a bed, office chair, shoes and tilt table. But remember, you can't buy yourself healthy. What you can hope for it to help the improvement you've already seen through exercise, paying attention to your posture and getting treatment.

Anyway, I recommend that you check out things on websites such as http://www.expertreviews.co.uk and https://www.which.co.uk as well as magazines such as *Which?*. Make the research a part of the process of buying things. If you need a little more guidance, go online and search for "good bed", "love my bed", "comfortable mattress" and similar phrases. Don't forget to read the warnings! Use the knowledge and experience of others so that you don't have to make their mistakes. Do this *before* you pay, because as soon as you've paid, you've handed over the power to the salesman.

Whenever you buy something, always make sure you get a proper receipt, names on salesmen (it's often on the receipt, but not always), and all promises in writing. Personally, I scan in all my receipts for over 500 pounds and put them in a folder on my Google account.

There are a lot of rules that all salesmen need to follow. Use this website: https://www.gov.uk/consumer-protection-rights to find out the laws and rights.

There are literally thousands of places to buy pain killers and ergonomic products in, but some good places are:

* Osmond Ergonomics, https://www.ergonomics.co.uk
* Posturite, https://www.posturite.co.uk
* Online Ergonomics, https://www.online-ergonomics.co.uk
* Adapt UK, http://adapt-uk.com/
* DS Ergonomics, http://www.ds-ergonomics.com

Beds

When it comes to beds, it's a jungle out there. Thickness, firmness, colour, material, mattresses, pillows, duvets, temperatures, prices and so on. The salesmen also count on you listening without questioning anything they're saying. Will you? A common stunt they pull is to try to split up the cost over 15 years, so that the price only ends up being a few pence each night – but the damn thing still costs 5,000 pounds! A budget alternative is to buy a regular springmattress from any furniture shop and then add on a mattress made of a material that eases the strain. The salesman will insist that the thicker this material is, the better you will sleep. According to my experience, approximately 7 cm will be plenty. Insist on borrowing the mattress for a week before you buy anything. Also insist that the pillow should be included if you buy the mattress.

For most people, this is enough. Your attitude is more important than the specific bed you're sleeping in. Because you:

* Don't worry about the bed.
* Don't spend too much money.
* Don't only test the bed – insist to bring it home for a week!

Bigger businesses are often easier to deal with since they have more margins to spare. If you're unhappy with the bed, you can get your money back. Smaller businesses don't have the option of being as generous. But most of the time, the law is on your side when returning the bed after a set trial period.

Office chairs

Considering how much time you're most likely sitting down, it's important that your back can keep its natural S-curve. I really hope that you didn't just buy the cheapest chair that is barely adjustable in height or has a back rest, but that you actually invested in an office chair where you can sit without more pain.

Most shops and websites that deal with ergonomics have chairs, but they cost a little more (between 500 and 1,500 pounds). On the other hand, it may be worth it if you spend a lot of time sitting. However, I don't think you should be paying more for the chair than the bed. A little different office chair is *Ergositter* (http://www.ergositter.net). There's a space between the sitting cushion and the back rest, which reduces strain on your back since your spine can sink in there.

Test the chair for at least *five minutes* before you make up your mind. That means that you have to exclude some chairs based only on how they look and practical details such as arm rests (which it should have). Never mind what the chair feels like when you sit down. Sit down and talk or read in the chair and when five minutes have passed – feel whether you're in more pain or the same. If you're feeling better – then the chair is okay.

It's a good idea to also buy a foot rest, so that your lower half gets to rest when you're sitting down. That means you don't need to cross your legs to sit steadily. The foot rest is meant to help you keep your feet parallel to the floor.

Shoes

Good shoes don't need to be expensive and you need a pair of shoes that aren't worn down to avoid making your back pain worse. Look at these things when you're buying shoes:

* The heel cap on the shoe (the part behind the heel) is meant to keep your heel in an upright position.
* The heel should be well-shaped – but not hard – and equally wide as the heel cap. Absolutely not high heels.
* The part of the shoe that is underneath your foot pad (where your toes are attached) should be flexible.
* The insole should have the same shape as your foot, to support the arch of your foot (but you can also get specific insoles from a foot specialist).
* You should be able to move your toes when you're walking.

A lot of people ask about *MBT-shoes*. MBT-shoes (acronym for ”Masai Barefoot Technology”, since the inventor looked at how the Masaai people were walking when he created the shoe) are very rounded underneath and almost look thick. The sole is also ”unstable”, which means that the body has to work to keep itself in balance. The effect is that the shoes force you to walk differently to take strain off your back. The inventors say that you get a workout at the same time, but there's little research that support them, but before you get a pair, speak to a back expert. After all, they do cost a few hundred pounds. Check out http://se.mbt.com/ for more information.

Tilt boards

The effect of spinal traction (relief for your back) is debated, but the majority of my thousands of patients experience that the symptoms improve whenever I use the tilting board. A tilting board is a kind of bench that you lie on and then lean so that you're on your back with your head down, strapped in by your feet. You've probably seen them if you've been in contact with a physiotherapist, naprapath or chiropractor. I use a *Mastercare Mini* at home too. It's easy to put it away when not in use, see:

http://mastercare.se/?option=com_content&task=view&id=100&Itemid=229. The tilting board removes strain off your back, neck, shoulders, knees and hips and could be an investment (be ready to spend approximately 500 pounds).

How you get the best deal

Tourist: "How do you get to Carnegie Hall?"

New Yorker: "Practice, practice, practice."

– *OLD JOKE*

In Sweden, most people aren't used to haggling, but it is possible. The trick is to practice, so that you don't try with a bed worth 5,000 pounds for the first time, because the chances to succeed then are very small.

Most people never bother practising and it's a little embarrassing in the beginning, but you get over it quickly. This is how you do it:

1. It's important that you start somewhere where you're in direct contact with the salesman/owner, and not in the supermarket, where the cashiers are stuck if change is missing. A market is perfect, because they're used to people haggling. Go there a little before closing time.

2. Add several products together that cost at least 75 pounds – and set the goal for the price ending up below 50 quid. Be

ready with another higher back-up price. The reason for why you should choose several products rather than just one, is that the salesman will see it as less money. People count in percentage more often than they think.[60]

3. Look at their first price as a suggestion. Ask what kind of discount they can give you. That means it's up to them to suggest a new price. Other questions you can ask are: ”What do I need to do to (reach the goal)?”, ”Have you made any exceptions before?” or ”But if I remove this item (so that it's still more than 50 pounds), what would you charge then?”

4. Counter their suggestion with suggestions of your own. Avoid being too pushy and try to seem reasonable. You do this by listening to the salesman's counter argument and then asking if the most important thing isn't to sell something at all. (”You won't make any money if you don't sell anything.”, for example.)

5. This is the hardest step: If you get a ”no” or can't even reach your back-up price, walk away! You don't need to be rude but show that you're not ready to pay the asking price.

To walk away is more difficult than any of the other steps, but it's important because it shows that you're serious. Otherwise, you've been pretending to haggle. If you've never walked away from one of these negotiations, then you haven't asked for a big enough discount. If that's the case, try lowering the price even further. You'll feel it as you walk away, but in the long run it will be better for you. Once you've practised a few times so that you feel comfortable, you can move on trying to do the same thing with a bed salesman: Put together a package of several items, have the goal of lowering the price by 30% and don't accept the asking price or any other price above your back-up price, but instead walk away. Be ready with cash and your chances of succeeding will be bigger.[61]

---

60 Research shows that if you receive the same amount of pounds in discount when you buy an expensive product (a laptop for example) as when you buy a cheap product (like a book), people like the discount on the cheap product more. That's why you shouldn't only think about it in percentage, but also on how many pounds or pence cheaper a discount makes the item you're buying. Use that for other things too.

61 More tips on how you can negotiate better prices, things and a lot of other stuff

Use new technology to get rid of stress

It's hardly a controversial thing that technology has changed our lives for better and worse. There's a lot to say if we start with the things that have gotten worse. For example, it's not good for your stress levels to be online all the time.

Already in the 1980s Stephen R. Covery wrote about how phone interruptions made it almost impossible to work efficiently. It's even worse now that people have phones (with text messages, mails, status updates from Facebook and Twitter) with them all the time. This is called the *24-hour society*, when you're always available and never offline. The consequences are tiredness, stress, bottled up emotions and later on physical ailments such as stomach ulcers and back pain. Scientists have even said that internet addiction is classified as a psychiatric disorder.[62] Thousands of people suffer from this every year.

Start by testing yourself. How do you do without technology for 24 hours? Can you manage two days? If not, you're addicted. How can you get away from all of that? The solution is to take control over your emails, phone, internet and computer games. It only needs to take approximately 30 minutes a day and it will *reduce your stress with at least 50%*. Do this by following these three steps:

1. Collect everything online

Nowadays, there are a lot of options for gathering your life online. There are a lot of advantages in this: You don't need to worry about anything disappearing *when* your computer breaks, you'll access it from your phone even when you're not at home, and you don't need to log onto several accounts.

Redirect all mail addresses to one. Most modern mail systems will allow you to save all the emails you'll ever receive. I prefer Gmail (http://mail.google.com), that is Google's mail function. I can collect my photos, calendar, documents and so on there, both securely and free. I check that mail twice a day. I then

can be found in Roger Dawson Secrets of power negotiating, Career press, 2001

62 According to New Scientist: http://www.newscientist.com/article/mg19726495.400internetaddictionisapsychiatricdisorder.html

answer to emails directly. This means that I can avoid a lot of stopping and starting throughout the day, which means that I actually have time to get things done – and this reduces stress.

2. Only allow a few people to get through to your phone

Decide what 2-3 people that need to be able to contact you 24/7. For me, it was my wife and my kids' day care. Everyone else will be passed on to the answering machine. This is what you do:

- Go onto your contact list on your phone.

- Mark those people who are allowed to get through to you with "Emergency Bypass".

- Mark everyone else with "Send to answering machine" or "Signal Off".

This will make your phone quiet down a lot more. You'll especially not have to deal with a lot of "where are you?" nonsense that can be heard everywhere. In the beginning, it was a little tough to get used to not being available 24/7, but this isn't about shying away from work or being lazy, it's about prioritising the things that are important in life.

Then decide two or three times a day when you'll be checking your answering machine. Phone back the important people and ignore the rest. People will learn soon enough that they can't reach you immediately and they'll start taking their own initiatives. That's a good thing. Put your phone in your bag instead of in your pocket, that way you won't be as tempted to check if someone has phoned.

3. Write auto messages

To show people that you're still alive, you can set your mail program to sending auto messages as soon as someone emails you. I've got this email:

"Hi,

Since I'm so busy at the moment, I'll only be answering emails twice a day, at 11:00 and 15:00. I'll also check my answering machine at those times, so if you've tried to contact me, I'll get back to you then.

This makes me both more efficient and productive and it means I can give you a better service.

Kind Regards,

Robin Wakeham"

Adjust the message so it suits you, and then record a similar message on your phone. Let them know your email address and ask them to write. It's much faster to reply to emails than to phone people and try to chase them down. And it forces them to put down what they want in words. Answer them as short and efficiently as you can.[63]

Count on it taking some time before you're comfortable with this change. Up to one month of withdrawal is not unusual, but it could take even longer depending on how addicted you are. Hang in there by following the advice in the back challenge on page 80.

It's important to *cross stuff off* your list that you don't "have to" do. When you cross things off, you'll experience a feeling of loss of control, but you were never fully in control anyway. You've always chosen what you want to do. Now's your chance to choose things with your back in mind. Your back does better with less stress.

But why do you only bring up the bad things about the new technology? The effects depend on how you use the technology! Hundreds of thousands of people have already found cool things to do relating to their health *with* this new technology.

63 If you want more tips on how you can make your life easier, I recommend Timothy Ferriss' book The 4hour work week, 2008/2009. Another book about this is The Power of Less by Leo Babauta, Hyperion, 2008.

Internet

Since the 1980s and 90s when internet became available and you actually had to be careful, internet was the best way to get something done efficiently. Don't miss the advantages with internet, just because you suspect that there are negative sides too.

For most people, the first point of access to internet is a search engine or a search box where they can write what they want to search for. The programs that operate these search engines are often very sophisticated. That's why you get better results the more detailed you are. It's better to write: "My back hurts, especially my lower back, but it also radiates out to my arm". Google and Yahoo, that are the two biggest search engines will sort through the results based on how many other people visited these sites and that's a pretty good measurement on what a believable website is.

Another access point is if you already know some websites that have useful information. You've gotten some tips about this in the book. I like https://www.nhs.uk.

Always look at who's behind the information. There are websites online that are dishonest and that write information without any reliable sources. I recommend that you always look for a link to "to this site" or similar, where it says who has written the content.

Internet forums are something that many women on maternity leave have discovered the point of. You can share experiences such as tips about solutions on problems and humour. http://www.friendsandfamilyforum.com is one of the most common ones, but there are several of them focused on people with different ailments.

Mobile applications

In many parts of the world, including Asia and Africa, they use mobile phones to the same extent that we Europeans and Americans use computers. Nowadays, the differences between them are smaller than you'd think; A pretty common mobile phone has so many functions that you need half a day to orient yourself when you buy it.

Applications ("apps", programs with usually one function) are what a lot of people think about when a phone is meant to be a helper. There are a lot of good apps to get in shape for example. An app like that works as a bad digital conscience that reminds you of when you need to exercise, specifically do push ups, so that you can learn to do a hundred push ups in just a few weeks. Other apps improve your sleep, like for example: http://www.lexwarelabs.com/sleepcycle/ that analyses your sleep cycle and wake you up during the right time so that you feel more rested.

The market for apps is huge, but it will likely grow further, so that apps specifically for people with back pain will be available. I'll include tips for these on:

http://www.ryggvarksexperternaljuger.se/ whenever they turn up, so keep your eyes open for more updated tools.

Computer games

Is there anything as misunderstood as computer games? I hardly think so. When the debate of video violence died out in the 1980s, a lot of people moved on to complain about computer- and videogames instead. It's not until the last few years that it's started to become acceptable for adults to play computer games too.

I play Nintendo Wii, a sort of computer game where you can connect all kinds of consoles: Steering wheels, remote controls, guns and – my favourite – boxing equipment. Me and my kids work up a sweat together when we play. It's both sweaty and fun, so I can't think of a better form of exercise. Who said that playing games had to be a passive activity?

***

I really want to encourage you to make use of these options, and similar tools. There's no reason to reinvent the wheel when we can connect online through internet, phones and games. Soon enough, new tech advances will turn up and the ones suffering from back pain will take on those too. To close your eyes to them will not benefit anyone.

Inconvenient Back Challenge Nr. 11

Since some previous inconvenient back challenges have taken several weeks and months, this one will seem easy. And it may be. But it's still important and will be very meaningful from here on and I can almost guarantee that you haven't done this before.

This is about thinking about yourself. But you're not just going to think any old thoughts:

Choose a reoccurring daily activity, for example when you brush your teeth or when you're in a lift. During that time, give yourself some attention. It doesn't need to be compliments, but it should be about you. Push away all thoughts about other people and focus on your goals, your body, your feelings and so on. What do you think? Give yourself permission to think selfishly for at least those few minutes. The rest of the day you can focus on everyone else, but these few minutes are just for you.

When you do this, you'll realise that you don't need others' attention as much as you used to, You'll handle it better if you ever get ignored or even criticised. It'll also be easier for you to discover what you want, something that is among the most important things you can do. Not to speak of how much easier it will be to do a 80/20 analysis!

And you've only got one more boulder left in your backpack. Is it starting to feel lighter?

This is how you get the most out of your back expert

Not only massage and exercises

Choose your back expert carefully

It's impossible to prevent all kinds of back pain no matter how well you prepare. If you're still in pain, then it might be time to keep looking and find a back expert.

Never forget that you're the one choosing which back expert to hire. It's best that way, since no one cares as much about your wellbeing as you do. Considering how many alternatives there are, you may need some help to find out which back expert to choose.

Most people who suffer from back pain go to an expert that their friends or family recommended. Maybe they don't know anyone else, or how to find out about what other options are available.

I wonder if they do the same thing when they buy a new car. Do they choose the same car dealer and model as their neighbour? Have they asked the neighbour if he or she has tried other car dealers? Has he or she researched the entire car market for the right model? You don't base a car purchase on just rumours or what your friends and family say. And still, a car is something you can change. Your back is something you're stuck with your whole life. Why aren't people as intelligent when it comes to choosing a back expert as they are when they buy a car?

One explanation is that there aren't any lists ready with good and bad back experts. Not everyone who treats backs are equally competent. Sure, you can find out if your back expert has been warned by the General Medical Council, or even gotten their license recalled – but that takes time and doesn't give you a very good image of each back expert. There are other aspects than competence that are important.

I did two big mistakes as a patient:

> One of them was that I didn't spend enough time finding the right back expert.
>
> The other mistake was to continue seeing a back expert that I didn't like or trust – and that didn't treat me with respect and dignity.

Those mistakes cost me a lot of time, energy and frustration. My own patients have confirmed that they've made the same mistakes. You can't imagine how many people keep seeing a doctor or physiotherapist that they don't like – or that makes several mistakes. They also voluntarily go to a back expert that extends the time they are in pain and are suffering from back problems, for no good reason. As I said, there are a lot of other options.

I can help you find the right back expert. But the choice of spending time choosing the right thing and maybe leaving a back expert you're not comfortable with is yours. You choose who to hire.

Which back expert should you see?

There are a lot of people that treat back pain: general doctors, physiotherapists, chiropractors, naprapths, orthopaedics and so on. The list goes on and on. I understand that that's confusing. So, how do you know who you should book an appointment with?

Your decision isn't made any easier by each one of the experts having their own expertise. In other words, the "right" back expert depends on what kind of back pain you are experiencing. Usually however, you can organise the experts according to what field they belong. I'm listing the most common treatments here, in the order you should see them:

1. Get to the closest hospital immediately if you're experiencing any of the following acute back pain symptoms:

* You can't control your bowels.
* You have decreased feeling in your genital regions.

* You're having difficulty getting an erection.
* Your legs and feet are weak.
* The back pain wakes you up at night or gets worse the longer you rest.
* You've been in a major accident, such as a car crash.
* The pain is unbearable.

2. Make an appointment with your GP.

The GP will examine your back and refer you to an orthopaedist if you need one. The general practitioner will also exclude serious problems, prescribe pain killers, recommend exercises and things you should avoid doing during this acute phase. However, they rarely give any specific exercises or general advice on how you should look after your back. To find your GP, go to: https://www.nhs.uk. If your general practitioner only gives you pain killers or asks you to rest, you should see another doctor. The rest and the medication could make things worse.

3. Make an appointment with a manual therapist (physiotherapist, chiropractor or naprapath)

A manual therapist can give you immediate treatment for your back pain. They are not allowed to prescribe any pain killers, but they can do a more thorough examination and give you treatment to ease the pain, increase mobility and strengthen your back muscles. They can also give you tailor made exercise programs, manual therapy, ergonomic advice and so on. Visit http://www.contactphysiotherapy.co.uk/manual-therapy.htm or http://www.physio.co.uk/treatments/physiotherapy/manual-therapy/.

Make sure that the person has their ID, by visiting the HCPC (Health & Care Professions Council) website:

https://www.hcpc-uk.org/aboutregistration/professions/index.asp?id=11.

If your pain is minimal, it may be enough to take a few walks, make a 80/20 analysis and have some relaxing massage.

Don't take up the time of manual therapists if that is the case but contact a massage therapist instead.

4. If your pain continues for more than four to six weeks, make sure you visit a back specialist.

See your GP for a follow-up appointment. If your problems are difficult, you will be referred to an orthopaedist, neuro surgeon, neurologist or pain doctor (they won't see you unless you have been referred). A back orthopaedist is a specially educated doctor. They can perform more in-depth examinations to give you a better diagnosis. Back surgeons have the following website https://spinesurgeons.ac.uk/, and orthopaedists have the following https://www.boa.ac.uk in the UK.

You can also look for a private back expert that preforms surgery but be ready for this to cost a lot of money. Since the organisations and clinics vary, it's best to search "private" plus the service you are looking for online or ask for advice from your GP or back expert.

How do I find the right back expert?

When you've chosen where to start, the hunt for a back expert that you like begins. Make sure that the back expert you choose to spend your time, energy and money on has a proper education, treats you respectfully and has treated many back pain patients successfully in the past.

Thanks to internet, these kinds of back experts are easier than ever to find. But we start "old school" by checking with people we know with paper and pen:

1. Ask your GP for recommendations

No matter if you've just moved to a new town, have been forced to change back expert or if you've never experienced back pain before, you should first of all use all the knowledge your GP has. When your general practitioner is checking so that there is nothing serious wrong with your back, you can take the chance to ask for recommendations for good back experts. Write these names down on a list.

2. Ask friends for recommendations

I hinted at the fact that you shouldn't trust your friends' and family's opinions. But you can still use their suggestions as a starting point. Write down the names of the back experts you're recommended on the same list.

3. Search online for recommendations

Search online with the following phrases:

* ”good back doctor”
* ”best back doctor”
* ”love my back doctor”
* ”back expert”
* ”back pain expert”

plus your area. Write down the names with the best reviews.

4. Do a specific search online

Write in the names you've collected, one at a time in a search engine such as Google or Yahoo, and you may find more reviews and information. Especially look for:

* things that *increase* the credibility – awards, dissertations, books, videos, work in bigger hospitals, media appearances and recommendations by other experts
* things that *lower* the credibility – criticising books and dissertations, ironic ”prizes”, questionable phrases and words such as ”homeopathy”, ”quant-” and ”you choose to be sick” or gaps in his or her resumé.

The official website for back experts is rarely the best place for objective reviews. You'll mainly find positive statements here.

5. Visit comparison-sites

There are several websites that focus on comparing competing services, here are some good ones in the UK:

* https://www.doctify.co.uk
* https://www.findoc.co.uk
* https://www.gp-patient.co.uk
* https://www.cqc.org.uk

Search for each back expert or clinic. Cross off the worst ones off the list and phone the best ones.

6. Book an appointment with the best back experts

Phone everyone you'd like to visit and book in a first appointment. Ask how long the general waiting time is. Notice how the receptionist speaks to you, since you'll be seeing them too.

7. Check if you get along with the back expert

Since you're going to spend quite a bit of time with your back expert, it's important that you feel comfortable with him or her. Do you perceive this person as competent? Are you being treated respectfully? Do you have the same humour? Are the facilities comfortable? Are you getting the time you need or is the back expert rushing through the appointment? If you don't like it, *don't book any more appointments*. You shouldn't see a back expert you don't get along with.

What other treatments are there?

It's not easy to know which treatments are alright, and which ones are sketchy. You'll find a clear overview of the most common ones here. Always see an accredited practitioner.

Back cracking

Chiropractic – from "cheir" (Greek, 'hand') and "praxis" (Greek, 'do'), "to do by hand".

Chiropractors today are highly educated (at least 5 years' worth of full-time studies), accredited and organised. In the UK the organisation is called British Chiropractic Association (BCA, https://chiropractic-uk.co.uk, phone number: 0118 950 5950). The American organisation is called American Chiropractic Association and can be found on http://www.acatoday.org/.

During the early 1950s, thorough examinations of the spine, showed that treatments of the spine, such as chiropractic or osteopathy could ease some of the pain. It's alright to use chiropractic or osteopathy to ease back pain. But if you believe that it can be used to treat everything from asthma to cancer, then you're shooting yourself in the foot. Not only does it hurt, it's completely useless when trying to get rid of your back pain.

Now to the warnings: One of the chiropractic treatments that is life threatening is "the quick neck crack". By quickly twisting the patient's head to the side, you can easily damage the veins that are found in the throat and thereby cause inner bleeding.

Immediately go to the emergency room if you experience the following symptoms during/after the treatment:

1. Difficulty pronouncing words (dysarthria)
2. Difficulties swallowing (dysphagia)
3. Vertigo (if the balance organ in your inner ear isn't working properly, this could cause vertigo.)
4. *Drop attacks* (sudden but very quick passing out effect on

your consciousness. You fall over but can get up immediately. Sign of temporary circulation disturbance in the brain stem.)

How often do these accidents happen? The full extent of the risks isn't fully known, but the risks are probably smaller than using pain killers. Considering that the doctor's oath says to not injure the patient further, and that I would never use this technique on my wife (always a good test), I'm personally doubtful and don't use the neck crack anymore. There are "kinder" methods where you get the same effect. However, other back experts have other opinions.

You're also at greater risk if you've recently had a baby, are taking birth control pills, are having problems with your circulation or high blood pressure, have neck problems/neck injuries or have previously had a stroke.

Think along these lines

1. Minimise risks for complications by only letting accredited physiotherapists/chiropractors/naprapaths treat you.

2. It's unfortunate, but there are still people that call themselves chiropractors even without a permit, in spite of this being illegal since 2006. Check your chiropractor through the GCC, General Chiropractic Council in the UK on phone number: 020 7713 5155. Those of you that are chiropractors and are reading this and are boiling from anger now: realise that I'm trying to help you by removing this insecurity that we're still closing our eyes to. If I were a chiropractor, I would put this information on my wall along with a phone number to the GCC to assure my patients. The debate about chiropractic will most likely continue for a long time.

3. Chiropractors aren't the only people that perform the neck crack, but some physiotherapists and naprapaths do it too. There's no reason to only blame the chiropractors. No matter which field your back expert belongs to, and especially if you're at greater risk as mentioned above, you should always make sure your back expert informs you in advance about:

a. What he or she is planning on doing

b. The risks of the treatment

All serious back experts are open with the risks, and not only the advantages.

Another danger is related to children: Children's backs are not done growing. They should never be exposed to manual treatment! Notify the Parliamentary and Health Service Ombudsman in the UK (https://www.ombudsman.org.uk).

Acupuncture

Acupuncture – from "acus" (Latin, 'needle') and "puncture" (Latin, 'punctured'), "to puncture with needle"

Acupuncture was invented in China several thousand years ago and was approved as a treatment for back pain in 1984 in Sweden. Still, the effect hasn't been completely proven. I've seen the effect of what's called the scalp acupuncture (needles on the top of your head) and it's convincing. Several people have passed out and many people have become dizzy. You'll get an even greater effect if you use acupuncture combined with other forms of treatment, such as manual treatment or exercise programs.

Science supports acupuncture as pain relief, possibly to the same extent as placebo (that is fake treatments) or possibly slightly more than that.[64] No one really knows why. Maybe it has to do with the fact that the needles bring out the body's natural morphine, the endorphins? There are no signs of the meridian theory actually working. (The theory was formed before the Chinese started to dissect people and consists of some wild guesses.)

I would never pressure anyone into acupuncture. And I only use acupuncture to ease pain – never to cure ailments or allergies.

The risks with acupuncture are fairly small, as long as you use single use needles from sealed packages and go to a practitioner who has a proper education. There is no accreditation for acupuncture

64 Both the usage of fake needles and placing them in the wrong places have been tried.

practitioners today, and if you go to someone who only does acupuncture you also have to pay the entire cost yourself including VAT, since the treatment isn't included in healthcare treatments.

Go directly to the emergency room if you're experiencing any of the following symptoms during/after treatment:

1. Chest pains and difficulty breathing, shallow breathing, followed by worry and tiredness (punctured lung)
2. Respiratory distress, blue or purple coloured skin and mucous membranes, especially your lips (punctured heart)
3. Fever, tiredness, nausea, no appetite, pressure over your right ribs, and muscle- and joint pains as well as skin rashes, yellow-coloured eye-whites, dark urine, light coloured faeces (hepatitis/liver inflammation)

Especially people who have previously had jaundice or liver inflammation or have liver inflammation in your family should avoid acupuncture. Hepatitis is life threatening.

Think along these lines

1. The majority of all accredited physio therapists, naprapaths and some chiropractors also have an education in acupuncture. Minimise the risks for maltreatment by visiting professionals that are accredited by UKAS, United Kingdom Accreditation Service.
2. If you still decide on seeing an acupuncture practitioner, you can find practitioners in the area you live in the UK through the British Acupuncture Council, https://www.acupuncture.org.uk/ or The British Medical Acupuncture Society, http://www.medical-acupuncture.co.uk.
3. No matter who is treating you, ask to see the needles that the acupuncture practitioner will be using. Insist that he or she only uses single use needles from unopened packages. Anything else would be as stupid as having a one night stand

with someone you don't know without using a condom. You risk hepatitis (liver inflammation) or HIV.

Massage

Massage from ”massage” (French, 'friction from kneading')

Massage isn't as risky as manual treatment or acupuncture, but it could be a good alternative if you are feeling tense and stiff – or if you just want to relax for some time. If you want to get rid of bigger problems related to back pain, you ought to choose something that works better, for example reducing stress or visiting an accredited back pain expert.

Massage is meant to among other things affect your autonomic nervous system, that is the part you can't affect with will alone. At the same time your blood circulation will increase, swelling will be reduced and scar tissue is prevented.

Just about everyone thinks this feels good, but some people find the situation a little strange at first. Just being touched is something most people long for and miss so much that they feel stressed out. If that's the case, massage can be part of the solution. Kerstin Uvnäs-Moberg, doctor and professor in physiology, has become world-known for her research that has proven that the ”love hormone” oxytocin is evoked by touch alone and has incredible effects on both the body and the mind.

I've seen people that refuse to open up to anyone but their massage therapist but tell them everything from sexual abuse they've been exposed to in the past to what it's like to be part of the Hell's Angels.

There are a lot of different types of massage, but in Sweden the *classical Swedish massage* is the most common one. The massage therapist alternates between strokes, kneading, circular movements and pounding. A treatment like this lasts 45-60 minutes and can cost anywhere between 40-60 pounds depending on where you are in the country.

Another massage treatment that is becoming popular is the *Thai-massage* ('nuat phaen boran'). This massage includes stretches and deep massage as well as certain yoga poses. The person that is receiving the massage wears clothes and is often lying on the floor, and the massage therapist uses hands, elbows and feet.

You shouldn't use massage as the only form of treatment for back pain. I've had patients that have tried this during several years. It's cost them a lot of money and has given them very little. Unfortunately, the short-term relaxation does not give you a pain free back long term.

There's also the dark side to the massage industry. That's the people that present complicated sketches of the human body and claim that massage on one body part can solve problems that are rooted somewhere else. Those connections between body parts are completely made-up. For example, zone therapists claim that there are connections between certain parts of your feet and the rest of your body, so that you can press one point under the foot and get physical reactions in a pre-determined point in another part of the body. The wizards Penn & Teller did a spot-on parody on the basic idea of zone therapy when they fixed a broken spark plug on a car by knocking on one of the tires with a wrench.

The tests that have been done clearly show that massage is nice and relaxing, but hardly anything else. And why does it have to be? We need more calm and rest, us back patients.

Think along these lines

1. The basic idea of the majority of the massage techniques are to reduce stress and get you to relax. If you can't relax, the massage doesn't really matter.

2. Make sure that you can trust your massage therapist by making an appointment through https://www.therapy-directory.org.uk where you can also find more information. You can also phone the Therapy Directory on 0333 325 2505. There are a lot of individual massage therapists too, and they usually have a good education and good treatments. You can also usually find good massage therapists in spas and wellness centres.

3. You know yourself best and you have to have the courage to clearly say how you want things. For example, if you are

a woman and know that you can only relax 100% when you have a male massage therapist, then you should clarify this when you make an appointment. If you can't get the right help, change massage therapist.

4. You won't feel any kind of deep relaxation if you and your massage therapist talk throughout the session. A good massage therapist will let the client control the conversation during the treatment but will try to speak very little themselves. Clarify that you want it to be silent by saying: "I've really looked forward to some quiet time with massage". The massage therapist will get the hint. Let me tell you a little secret: Your massage therapist, hair dresser, the person who does you mani-pedi, basically everyone who takes care of people daily finds the silence "absolutely wonderful". Otherwise, they have the same 5-10 conversations all day long, one year after the other. The summary is as follows: You pay, so if you need to have a chitchat to relax, then go ahead: Talk till you can't talk any more. But don't sit and chitchat because you believe that the person treating you has a great interest in what you have to say or that you'll get a better treatment or price. Often, you'll get better and faster results if you keep quiet and let the person do his or her work undisturbed.

Meeting Sven-Erik

My clinic, 2002

He more or less walked straight into my room and crawled up onto the bed.

"You could give me some nice massage." (He didn't ask but stated or ordered it – I'm not sure."It's free for me anyway."

I walked up to him."That's not quite how it works. Hi, my name is Robin Wakeham. What do you say, Sven-Erik, should we start with a short examination?"

"I've already seen my GP and had an examination. Sometimes I get pain killers, sometimes I get sent home without them. This time, I was sent here."

”Good”, I replied. ”You said that you’ve seen your general practitioner many times. How long has your back been hurting?”

He snorted and sat up. ”Well, on and off for some ten years. My lower back.”

He noticed that I was looking at how he was sitting and hurried to add: ”I know that I’m sitting like a bloody sack of potatoes, but don’t touch me.” He started to look aggressive. ”I don’t have time to do all of the things I should be doing!”

”Why are you getting so worked up?” I said and remained calm. Angry patients are unfortunately not uncommon. ”Have I said or done anything?

He offloaded yet another rant and started complaining about people like me, who think that he has all the time in the world to spend on exercises and doctor’s appointments and buy this and that. I let him speak for a while. He didn’t have anything new to say. But finally, I realised that Sven-Erik wasn’t going to change unless he had to. Someone had to confront him, otherwise he was going to walk through life these next 15 years and cost himself and others time and money. I started softly:

”Serves me right”, I said and smiled. ”I hope you’re finished, because it’s my turn now. You say that your back is hurting. I suspect that it really hurts since you followed your GP’s recommendation and came here. Still, you think that some massage will take care of the problem. But, I can tell you what’s going to happen if you don’t change your attitude pretty soon: You’ve been getting warnings from your back for ten years now, probably because you’re sitting in an office, never exercise and still think that you can live like you did when you were 18 years old! The warnings you’ve gotten will only get worse for each year, and you’ll feel them more and more. In the end, you’re 90% likely to her a hernia, in other words, one of your discs in your back will break, or you’ll experience some other painful and serious problem. The merry-go-round is in session then! Because if you still aren’t ready to do anything to change your life, you will really ruin your back, and not to mention other things in your life that will be turned upside-down!”

I caught my breath and kept going before he had time to interject with an excuse: ”But, I’ll be here in case you decide that you want to find the cause of your back pain and do something about it.”

He stared at me for some time. Then he said: ”Is it really that bad?”

I thought about the ethic about scaring patients, but in Sven-Erik’s case, all attempts to down-play the risks would cause him to lose motivation. I decided to get straight to the point:”I think that you need to spend a few hours a week on fixing your back now, if you want it to work properly five years from now. I don’t really think you have a choice in this, unless you want to pretend like nothing. But then you know how that will turn out...”

Sven-Erik, who had been on fire at the beginning of the appointment was not sitting quietly thinking. I wonder if anyone had ever opposed him like that before.

But, I soon noticed that his stubborn personality that was a big part of the problem could be turned into something positive.

We quickly found the root of the problem. Together we created a solution that suited him.

***

Of course I don’t recommend raising your voice to all your patients. That kind of behaviour rarely leads to anything positive, and it’s also in an ethical grey-zone. The point is that a lot of people like Sven-Erik come and see me and other back experts – people that think t we will fix the problem for them without them needing to do anything. Some of them need a cold shower to get going with the things they need to be doing.

These people almost always know what they need to do. Yet, they haven’t done it. They make it sound like an enormous effort needs to be made, but often all they need is a small push in the right direction. If you know what buttons to push. That is, what the motivation is for getting them started.

Yoga

Yoga – from ”yóga” (Sanskrit, ‘to contorl’, ‘to steer’ or ‘to unite’, and other meanings)

The first description of yoga originated from 100 B.C. Nowadays, yoga can be found in more shapes and forms than you could imagine. With over 435 million practitioners all over the world, this is one of the world’s most practiced disciplines. They all have in common the fact that they are relaxation techniques, often with specific movements. The movements train your muscle strength as well as your stamina.

Many of the exercises that are used in yoga strengthen your back muscles and improve your flexibility, but you should be careful, especially as a beginner. Every year, thousands of people in the US are injured, from twisting and overstretching. As long as you take it easy in the beginning and gradually increase the difficulty of the exercises (but skip the worst ones), it should be fairly riskfree.

Breathing is also an important part of it to further increase the relaxation. By slowing down your breathing, you will be more focused and lessen your stress levels – with lowered blood pressure, decreased muscle tension and lower pain levels as a result. [65]

All in all, this is a treatment form that has many good effects on chronic back patients and has a low risk factor.

Think along these lines

1. Yoga is a form of workout among many others and it works well if you’re stressed or need better posture. You don’t need to buy all the talk (the philosophy behind it) or all the terms in Sanskrit. There’s no reason to change your entire life, just to get some exercise and relaxation. As long as you’re slowing down, you’re doing it right.

2. You can find a lot of yoga courses in the phone catalogue or online if you search for ”yoga” and your area, but it’s even easier to ask around people you know for some advice. Tell your instructor (avoid getting into some kind of humble

65 Loic Burn, Michael S. Sinel,WilliamW. Deadorff Treating your back & neck pain for dummies (2007), JohnWiley & Sons, Chapter 12

student-adept-role) what your goal is so that you can get specific help.

3. My personal favourites among the yoga techniques are MediYoga for back pain as well as Bikram yoga, for the stressful society. This takes place in 40 degree hot rooms. I've practised both of them many times and I enjoy them very much.

Warning signs at the first meeting

Once you've found the right back expert and want to get started with treatment, there are a few things you should keep in mind.

Part of the secret of getting the best help is in creating a good relationship with your back expert. His or her behaviour will partly be controlled by rules. That means that he or she needs to keep some distance. This in turn means that the responsibility is on *you* to make the relationship as good as it can be.

I'll tell you more here about what I've learned from thousands of patients.

There isn't one back expert that's right for everyone. I don't want to say who will be the best or worst back expert for you either. But, you should be sceptical and careful if:

* The back expert or the receptionist is being difficult with appointments and being on time. Some delays may occur, but if the delay is over 30 minutes and you haven't gotten an explanation or an apology, you have a good reason to leave. In that case, let the reception know why before you leave the clinic.
* The appointment starts with discussions about money.
* The back expert starts to treat you without first going through your medical history and preforming an examination.
* There are promises that the back expert will also cure other ailments with the same methods, especially if the method is said to cure cancer, genetic diseases and sicknesses caused by virus or bacteria!
* The back expert doesn't want to tell you how many treatments he or she thinks that you will need.
* You are advised to not ask for other back experts' opinions.
* Your back expert attempts to get your family and friends to come in for treatment.
* Something goes really wrong with the treatment and the back expert tries to get you to keep quiet about it, by for example not

charging you. He or she won't mention that you can notify the HCPC, Health & Care Professions Council.

If you were to bump into a back expert like this, walk away. Chances are that the treatment is both bad for you and expensive. Don't be tempted to accept bad behaviour. You're worth more than that.

Note that when you begin a treatment, you may experience more pain than before the treatment! Also remember that complicated ailments such as hernia could make it difficult to estimate exactly how many times you need to come in for treatment. If you've neither gotten worse nor better after 6-8 treatments, find another back expert.

How you prepare for your first appointment

The headline above may give you a clue, that you can't just wander in to see your back expert, but just in case, it may be better to make it clear here: Your back expert doesn't know you, he doesn't know anything about your problems, doesn't understand your humour or your way of speaking, has lots of other patients, a background of his or her own, have bad and good days and so on. That's why you have to do what you can to explain everything quickly and clearly. That's not an easy thing to do.

But there are some tricks you can use to make it easier for you:

1. Know where you have your papers

I'm sure you've received a lot of papers before – records, prescriptions, exercises, papers from the NHS and possible notes from other appointments. Keep all of them in a folder. Bring the folder with you.

2. Write down what you need to say

Write down the symptoms you've experienced (rated based on how severe they are), questions you might have, previous recommendations, the medication you're taking and what you think the appointment will result in. You can also bring a drawing of your body and mark where your back is hurting. You'll find out more about what questions you should ask in the next section.

3. Dress nicely

It's a shame, but it's true: How you look and behave dictate what kind of help you will receive. By dressing nicely (clean suitable clothes are enough) you'll make it easier for your back expert to come to the conclusion that you are a serious person that has done what you can to get rid of the back pain. And all clothes will naturally look better if you've had a shower before.

4. Leave home on time

Late patients have less time to make a good impression and to get help. Most of the time when people are late, it's because they have underestimated how long the journey takes. Make sure you have some extra time and a book to read instead of rushing in out of breath.

Also see page 52, you'll get more tips there.

Meeting the back expert

So, how do you say the right things within the first 10 seconds? Do this:

1. Take it seriously.

The more you prepare, the bigger the chances are that you will get the right help. Look at it like you would a job interview. Exactly, that's how important it is. To just show up and think everything will be okay is set-up for you to say something wrong.

2. Write down your symptoms when you experience them.

This is sometimes called a pain diary or journal. Note how severe the problems are, for example "Tuesday night, sharp pain in my lower back." A way of measuring pain is introduced on page 228.

3. Write down what you're going to say beforehand.

Write down *the strongest symptoms, important dates, all medications you are taking, names of other back experts or doctors you have seen, descriptions of what they have done, what effect it had as well as other important things such as MRIs or referrals* and so on. Look through your back bible (Inconvenient Back Challenge 1), so you're not forgetting anything.

I know that it seems silly to write these things down, but it's not any different from writing a grocery list before you go to the shop. Put numbers in front of each item depending on how important they are. If you've experienced pain down your leg, that's one of the things you should mention immediately, but don't have to mention that you slipped on some ice five years ago and that you believe this is a reoccurring pain from then.

Draw a man on a paper (or use the figure on http://ryggvarksexperternaljuger.se/figur) and mark out where you're most in pain, and where you're least in pain. It's a very good way to visualise the pain for you and your back expert.

4. Bring the note, your back bible and other important papers.

The note with symptoms and the important dates won't be of any use if you leave it at home. Neither will previous papers from your GP or other back experts. You have a back bible, bring it with you. That will impress your back expert.

Hopefully, all health care professionals will have made sure to get your complete records within a few years, but while you wait, you can do it yourself. A big advantage is that you have access to it at all times. Another advantage is that you don't have to do it more than once, which is a typical thing you learn when you think 80/20. In the UK you can access your health records through your GP or by contacting the clinics where you have been treated.

5. Then read your list with the most important things first.

Use the note as much as you need to when you're telling the back expert about your problems. He or she will appreciate that you're prepared. Don't hand over the note until you've gone through all the items you wrote down.

Besides making your ten seconds as full of facts as possible, you should also aim for making the back expert as curious as possible so that you get *more* than ten seconds. This is how you do just that:

1. Avoid saying "It started with...". The back expert will then assume that you're going to tell him or her the full story. You might as well say "Once upon a time...".

2. Instead, say "For about two weeks, I've had problems with...". By clarifying the point of time, you're showing that you didn't come in the first day you were in pain. The point is that you've tried to let your back heal on its own. You don't have to tell your back expert the exact time of the day the problem occurred, but it's a good idea to keep track of the dates.

3. Then mention the greatest problem from your list, and just how problematic it is. One tip: Your problem isn't the world's biggest problem, so don't try to make it sound like it is. Use the pain levels on page 228.

4. Either finish up right after this and let the back expert ask his or her questions – or mention something else that is equally problematic. If you have two equally big problems, mention them in chronological order: "Two weeks ago, I

started having stabbing pains in my lower back, more than regular back pain. A few days later, I realised that it was radiating out into my arm." Imagine that you're telling an exciting story, *but you can't exaggerate.*

List of questions for your back expert

What are the most important questions to bring up with your back expert? Here's some help:

To determine if you have a bad back expert

* Are you accredited?
* How long have you been practicing?
* Do you mainly treat back pain?
* What can you treat? (If they mention cancer and other difficult diseases, you should be careful.)
* What happens if you accidentally hurt me?
* Do you keep a record? (They should.)
* How do you feel about working with my GP?
* How many times do you think I need to come in? (Is the focus on you becoming better or on you coming back? Extra bonus if they're planning on making themselves redundant.)
* Could the problem be something else? (Listen for masters/gurus/favourite theories)

To get the best diagnosis

* Do you know what the cause of my back pain is?
* Do you think that anything in my background could have caused it?
* Could it be anything else?
* How severe is my back pain?

* How likely is it that my back pain will worsen?
* Do you have a lot of patients suffering from this?
* Do I need to do any tests?

To get the right recommendation

* What type of treatment would suit me best?
* Could you recommend any exercises that I could do at home?
* How long does it usually take before other patients with the same problem have recovered?
* Do they usually make a full recovery?
* What should I do if the treatment doesn't help and I'm not improving?
* How long does it usually take before the patient notices a difference?
* Could you give me an estimate for how long I will be seeing you?
* Can I still work?
* What can I do to avoid back pain in the future?

Pain levels

Pain is hard to measure and varies from one person to the next. That's why pain doctors and everyone who works with pain use the patient's own descriptions. Sometimes they may ask the patient to put a number on their pain between zero and ten. The different levels can then look like this:

Level 0: No pain.

It feels like normal.

A little pain 1-3

Doesn't get in the way of most activities. Psychological, medical and practical solutions can be found (such as cushions) to adjust in relation to the pain.

Level 1: Very mild pain

Very mild, barely noticeable pain, such as a mosquito bite or a stinging nettle. You usually don't think about the pain.

Level 2: Uncomfortable

A little pain, like pinching yourself on the arm with your nails.

Level 3: Tolerable pain

Highly noticeable pain, like a cut, a punch that gives you a nose bleed or a doctor that gives you a shot. The pain isn't so strong that you can't get used to it. After some time, you won't think about it.

Mediocre pain 4-6

Gets in the way of many activities. Demands that you change the way you live, but you're still independent. You can't get used to the pain.

Level 4: Painful

Strong, deep pain like an average tooth ache, the first pain from a bee sting or a minor injury such as hitting your toe really hard. So strong that you notice it almost all the time and can't get used to it.

Level 5: Very painful

Strong, deep and stinging pain, such as a twisted ankle or hitting your thumb with a hammer. Not only do you notice the pain all the time, but you're also thinking about limiting the pain so much that your life quality is decreasing. Temporary disturbances in your personality are common.

Level 6: Intensive pain

Strong, deep, stinging pain that is so strong that it's partly preventing the person from thinking clearly. At this level it's hard to work normally or be social. Comparable with a bad headache (the non-migraine kind) combined with several bee stings.

Severe pain 7-10

Unable to perform normal activities. Feeling handicapped and can't live independently.

Level 7: Very intense pain

Same as level 6, but the pain is preventing you from thinking clearly half the time. You become handicapped and can't live independently. Comparable with an average migraine attack.

Level 8: Really terrible pain

Pain that is so intense that you can't think clearly at all, and you often go through a bigger personality change if the pain has been continuous for a long time. Suicidal thoughts can occur. The pain is similar to giving birth or a very severe migraine attack.

Level 9: Extreme pain

The pain is so intense that you can't tolerate it and have to take pain killers or have surgery, no matter what consequences it may result in or the risks involved. If it doesn't work, suicide is common because there's no enjoyment in life. About the same level of pain as throat cancer.

Level 10: Unbearable pain

The pain here is so intense that you're almost passing out.

Most people have never experienced this kind of pain. Those who have experienced level 10, have been in a serious accident, crushed a hand or had severe burns, and lost consciousness from the pain rather than the blood loss.

What is the back expert thinking during the meeting?

Back experts start their examinations the moment you walk in by looking at how you move. Then he or she will continue to look, feel, ask you to bend and stretch, test and just generally bother you throughout the meeting. Both doctors and physiotherapists with education in this field are trained to examine different parts of the body to find the reason for your problems. We check out what's working and what isn't in your body, and that's why x-rays don't always give us enough information since they show your body in a resting state.

We also listen to what you say. We listen very carefully, because we know that some symptoms come and go. Often, symptoms don't show during the actual hospital visit. But more importantly. Our goal is to create a trusting relationship with you.

When we have excluded different options and come to a conclusion, we start by explaining to you what your problem is caused by. We put a lot of emphasise on this. Because, a lot of patients come to see us after a number of visits in other health care sectors without getting a proper understanding for what they are suffering from. Considering that they, and you won't have us looming over your shoulder for more than a small percentage of the time, it's important that you possess a good understanding of what's happening. You're the one who carries the main responsibility of the rehabilitation. The more we can get you to take that responsibility seriously, the easier it will be for both yourself and us.

Should you have surgery or not?

One of the most important and most common questions I get is; Should I go through surgery or not? There's no easy answer to that. You have to decide for yourself. What I can do is give you a few different points of view that you can discuss with your back expert.

Here are some statements. If you feel that you relate to one or the other more, you have a good foundation to make a good decision on.

Reasons to have surgery for your hernia

* You're experiencing difficult and crippling pain in your legs, numbness and weakness.
* The symptoms of your legs have not improved in spite of at least 4 weeks of medical treatment.
* You're getting signs/indications that the pressure on your nerve is worsening, that is you're experiencing an increased pain in your leg, increased loss of sensation, paralysation or increasing weakness, loss of coordination, complete loss of reflexes.
* Your work requires you to quickly gain back function in your back.
* You can follow a rehabilitation program during several weeks after surgery.
* Do you have any further reasons for why you want to have surgery on your hernia? If so, write them down.

Reasons to not have surgery

* You would like to get medical treatment that includes physiotherapy, exercise, rest and medication.
* There's no guarantee that an operation will ease your problems.
* There's no guarantee that the operation will have better results long-term if you compare it to medical treatment.
* There are risks of infection, pain and slow healing with surgery, and you may possibly need to have surgery again.

* All surgery includes risks of complications such as heart attacks.

The hernia test that will help you make a better decision

Go through the questions below and circle the answers that are true in your case. By doing this you will get a better idea of exactly how you feel about having surgery. Then bring this test to your doctor so that you can discuss the answers together. Doctor's visits can be very quick and it's not unusual that you may feel that you haven't gotten all the answers you wanted at the end of your appointment. You can't put the full blame on the doctors. You have to prepare in advance if you want to increase your chances of having a constructive meeting with your doctor where your questions will be answered and a treatment plan set up. The doctor will appreciate this and you'll make a better decision together regarding your hernia.

Answer "yes" or "no"

* The exercises I got from my doctor/physiotherapist to do at home seem to be helping my back.
* I've done the exercises I was given by my physiotherapist for 8 weeks but the pain is still the same.
* I'm taking the medication and it seems to help.
* My hernia has causes me pain, weakness and numbness for over 6 months.

Answer "yes", "no" or "unsure"

* I feel handicapped because of my hernia.
* I feel worried that I may need to have surgery again in a few years.
* I'm not feeling worried, and I feel okay about having back surgery.

What conclusion did you come to?

The purpose with the questions above, is to find out where you stand in this important decision. Circle the statement below that best corresponds with your decision. I know that this is difficult but it's very important that you make a decision and avoid stuffing your head in the sand and close your eyes to the problem at hand.

Leaning towards surgery   Leaning towards no surgery

Inconvenient Back Challenge Nr. 12

After having removed 11 boulders from your backpack over a fairly long period of time, it's finally time to empty the backpack completely! Imagine, how nice it will be...

When you are in pain, you're obviously very careful about not making it any worse. The down-side of it is panic and egoism, something that make it more difficult to become pain free. The only solution is that you pay attention to others. Not by not caring about yourself, but by caring about others as much as you care about yourself. This will give you charisma. It will also give you confidence and more energy.

During the next 30 days:

- When you meet someone, smile while noticing the person's eye colour (without staring of course).
- Give everyone you meet an honest compliment or positive comment. People care about what others think so they will start to listen to you more.
- Show that you enjoy spending time with that person.
- Refer to things that the person has mentioned previously.
- Find out what the person's interest is and ask questions about it.
- Give up the false shyness.
- Stop yourself any time you're about to fill a moment of thought with "er"sounds. In the beginning this will feel strange but pretty soon you'll speak more fluently and that will give people a thought through impression of you.

Living with back pain

The relationship with your back expert isn't everything in the world. At best, you'll see your back expert 1-2 times per week. The rest of the time you have to look after yourself. Some of that time you'll most likely have homework in the shape of exercises. Some of the time you'll be sleeping. What do you do with the rest of the time?

I hope that you won't be too surprised when I write this: What you do with the time affects how quickly you will recover or how much you will improve.

Are you starting to feel nervous?

Don't be. You've had that responsibility all along. The difference is that your focusing on it now, and that will give you better results. Besides, most of the continued life is just like before your back pain started.

In actual fact, the more you live like normal, the faster you will recover – assuming you lived a good life before. It's like a diabetic: They get to live about the same as before they were diagnosed with diabetes, but they have to eat better and more regularly and exercise more, and thereby get a reminder of their mortality. What more could you want?

Yes, of course, a guide for what you can and can't do. And how to do it. Here it is:

What you can't do

Few things are completely impossible when it comes to back pain. Some things are stupid to spend time doing, such as bungee jumping and car racing or a marathon with your favourite TV-show, but impossible? No.

If you're suffering from severe back problems, you may not want to do much, but that's a matter of motivation. You *can*, if you want to. The solution is in how you look at the problem.

Instead of thinking about what you can't do, I recommend that you think along the lines of "What can I do to do the things I want? That way you'll transform into someone who can do things. Others start to adjust around you and help you with the things you need help with.

Enough about limitations. No more narrowminded images of how you'll be stuck at home and can't ever attend parties any more. But you have to choose to want to.

Sex

That thing about "getting laid" must sound pretty good. And with all the physical and psychological benefits of sex, it may be a little easier convincing (or seducing) your partner to a tumble in the hay.[66]

But when you're suffering from back pain, sex is rarely the first thing on your mind. You're busy thinking about other things such as getting rid of the pain and all the other problems. Often, your sex drive is a priority somewhere below cleaning your colleague's cat's litter box.

And I can absolutely understand that, but remember, think in opposites. Research shows that sex works as a natural pain killer.[67] Your body becomes a little numb. You get rid of and decrease the pain for a short period of time.

You don't have to be really in the mood before sex either. Many sex experts agree that you may need to step over a threshold (just go for it) to get into a place where you're more in the mood. Occasionally you may be "faking" being turned on and have sex, and then it can sort of just keep going naturally.

Of course, *I don't mean* that you should feel forced to have sex. Force and sex do not go together. I would like to give you the tip of trying to find your erotic side again. I promise that you'll like it in the long run.

So, even if you're not in the mood, go for it anyway. This is how you can build up your feelings:

---

66 I hope that you don't have actual hay in your bed, since modern beds are much better for your back.

67 Psychology Today writes about it here: https://www.psychologytoday.com/intl/blog/paintracking/201111/thehealingpowerssex

Step 1: Dating

Decide on an erotic date that's adjusted after your back. Set aside plenty of time for this. Make it a priority. Prepare for the date in advance by texting or emailing each other and describing what you want to do.

Let the date be all about the senses – sight, hearing, smell, soft clothes, a good temperature in the room and good food.

Start by having a nice dinner (or swimming if you want to be adventurous). Make sure you get to be alone – get a baby sitter, turn off the phone, close the curtains, let the neighbours know you won't be home. Decide to not talk about things that stresses you out – all of that can wait.

Get dressed up. Prepare food with a lot of fruit and vegetables. Avoid fat and salt, as well as food from tins and packages, since that often makes you feel unsexy. Drink in moderation. Spread out a blanket where you want to create a nice atmosphere, preferably with candles and romantic music. Cushions may make it more comfortable for you.

Eat *slowly*, preferably with your fingers. Take turns describing what you like about each other. Treat each other to fruit or small pieces of chocolate, maybe in more creative ways (accidentally spill something on your body and let your partner eat it off of you).

Let your date move onto massage or a bubble bath. It will relax you and your back and it will also get you closer to each other physically without it having to become sexual too quickly. (Don't forget to drink water to replenish fluids, otherwise you may get a head ache and that's an immediate turn off.)

Step 2: Foreplay

If you are a man, you should read this section extra carefully. In this situation foreplay is even more important and most men aren't great at it.

Take it slow – fear of pain is as much of a turn off as the actual pain. By relaxing and taking it slowly, you're lowering the chances of your back starting to hurt when you're having the best time. But also take it slowly to extend and delay the pleasure. The longer it takes, the better the climax will be.

Keep talking to each other. Tell each other what you like to do and what you'd like the person to do to you. Also tell your partner what you think you should avoid to prevent pain. This is something both men and women are bad at, so get started with the descriptions. How sexy would it be if you let go of your inhibitions?

Touch each other a lot. The more excited the woman is before you move on, the smaller the chances are for the man to have an early ejaculation (something that happens to men every now and then). But touch is also a way for you to get physically closer to each other. Explore each other's bodies and alternate soft and hard strokes after the signals your partner is giving you.

Eroticism can be a helpful tool if the mood isn't naturally there, it should be a turn on for the both of you. And if you've prepared something in advance, it may be exciting to show each other what you find a turn on. If you don't want to buy erotic videos, I've heard that porn is available online.

Ste 3: Intercourse

You probably know this part pretty well already, so I'm only going to mention a few sex-related things for back pain patients.

Neither one of you need to be an acrobat for this. (And still I keep meeting patients that for some reason think they need to be.) Use cushions or rolled up towels if you need to.

But that doesn't mean you can't try out new positions and variations of what works for the both of you (there are several books only about sex for people with back pain, these have pictures that work both as instructions and inspiration[68]). Some easy positions you could try are the following[69]:

68 Two examples are Lauren Andrew Herbert Sex and back pain, Impacc USA, 1997 and Pierre Angier The joy of comfortable sex, Excelsior Books, 2007.

69 For the sake of space, I use ”men” and ”women", but these positions can of course be used by anyone, regardless of gender and sexuality. And yes, I am aware of the number of this footnote.

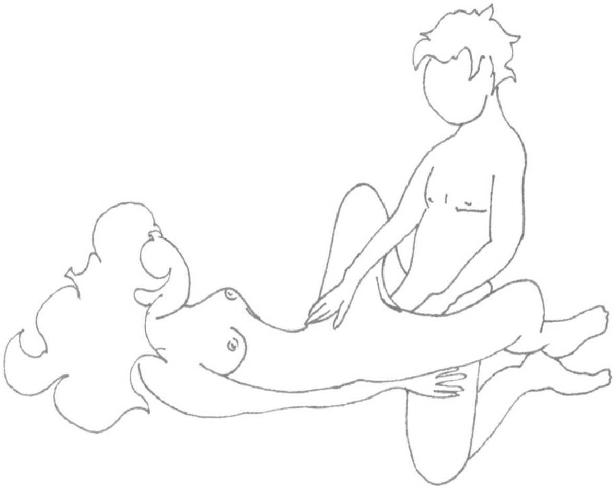

Image 1: The Missionary position but with pulled up legs. [70]

In case she is experiencing back pain, he can help by holding up the legs so that she doesn't have to tense her leg muscles. If the man is in pain, he should keep his spine straight and rock his entire upper body back and forth instead of thrusting with his hips. The woman can have a cushion under her bum to further help him.

Image 2: The woman *rides the man.* This position is especially good if the man is the one in pain. Put a pillow or rolled up towels behind the knees. If the woman is in pain, she can lean down towards the man so that her back is relaxed.

70 The images in this section are drawn by Marie Grahn.

Image 3. *The woman is sitting in the man's lap on a chair without arm rests – facing forwards or backwards.* If the woman is the one with a back pain, this position can make it easy for her to choose position and movement pattern by either moving her hips or her entire body. It's best to use a narrow chair and pillow under the man's bum.

Image 4. *The woman is sitting on a table and the man is standing in front of her.* The closer the woman is to the edge, the easier it will be. You can also use a chair, while the man is standing on his knees.

Image 5. *The couple is forming a T.* The man is lying under the woman's bent knees. This variation is easy for the woman, but possibly more difficult for the man.

If you're having problems

A lot of things need time well for it to work out like in the films (don't even try it!). You can't always succeed, but if you're having reoccurring problems, get some help. Relate – The Relationship People have a website https://www.relate.org.uk where you can find sex therapists in your area.

Have fun

Back pain doesn't have to mean that you need to feel down or can't have fun. On the contrary, this is the perfect time to have more fun than usual – to balance out some things if nothing else. Never mind, you don't need a reason to have fun. Just have as much fun as you can:

* *Watch comedies* – They're usually shorter than thrillers and romance, so you can get up and move quicker. Some of my favourites are Woody Allen and Seinfeld, but you may like something very different. Watch something with others if you can, it will make the experience better – and you'll have something to discuss afterwards that isn't related to your back(!). Also, don't forget about the option of watching really bad films.

* *Read books by fun authors* – By reading you get to use your imagination. Don't be scared to laugh out loud whether you're alone or on a bus. I promise, the mood will just get better – as long as you're not at a funeral, but then the book option seems to point towards the fact that you didn't like the person anyway, so maybe it is a suitable choice after all.

* *Make fun of yourself and your back pain* – You don't need to be a stand-up comedian or anything like that, but just let some of your frustrations come out with humour, it will at least make it easier for your friends and family. Try by finding 20 variations of ending the sentence "It hurts as much as..."

* *Collect humour*. It's easy to forget or lose the jokes you hear and read. Save them in a specific notepad.

* *Invite people to a party* – It's good for you to spend some time with people and have fun.

* *Sing karaoke*

* *Go to a concert, play or some other performance* – for example a stand-up comedy show.

Learn new things

I'm sure there are a lot of things that you've always wanted to learn: How to speak Italian, astronomy or accounting. There are lots of opportunities to do that in a nice package, without any pressure. That is some of the local or online courses near you. It costs very little money and you get to meet new people that share your interest. Courses start continuously and there are both long and short courses so that you can choose something that suits you.

Back pain and authorities

HOW YOU WIN THE BATTLE AGAINST INSURANCE COMPANIES, THE GOV.UK, JOBCENTRE PLUS, YOUR EMPLOYER AND OTHER AUTHORITIES – EVERY TIME!

No person that works for an authority or a business will feel sorry for you because you're suffering from back pain. They won't make your life any easier either. That's why this section is all about how to build your case, how to document, negotiate and knowing your rights and responsibilities and what to do when you get into trouble.

The secret behind it all is to be professional. I know how tempting it is to shout at the person behind the desk ”My back bloody hurts!”. But that would only hurt you and your chances for compensation or being treated well in the future. As a friend of mine used to say: ”If you're going to deal with hospitals, you need to be healthy”. The same goes for authorities and businesses in the same industry. If you are sick, you have to fake being healthy or make sure you get assistance by someone who is healthy. Or use this book to help you.[71]

Step 1: Protect your rights

As soon as you can (directly after an accident for example) it's time to start protecting your rights. What happens next depends on how you act from the beginning. The more organised you are, in spite of all the feelings and stress, the better you will do in the future.

71 The advice described in this chapter do not guarantee that you will receive benefits. Also, I'm not a lawyer than can help you win these proceedings. But I have time tested strategies that increase your chances if you follow the advice. This section is partly based on Joseph Matthews How to Win Your Personal Injury Claim, Nolo, 2009, above all others, Chapter 3.

Do this:

The keyword is documentation. Get as many papers and other information as you can. Here are a few examples of what you should do:

1. Write

Write down as much as you can, as quickly as you can before you forget anything. Note down everything you remember about the accident or the time your back pain started. What were you doing? Who was there? Where were you going? What happened during the accident? Write down all your impressions as carefully as you can. On my website http://www.ryggvarksexperternaljuger.se you can download all the documents you need to support you.

During the first D-Day, write down all your pains and marks that may be relevant. Note down lack of sleep, worry and other intangible things. Talk to others with the same problems so that they can become witnesses later.

How much money and other things have you lost because of the injury? Income loss, missed meetings, course opportunities and parties, cancelled holidays or other things that you've missed because of the injury. It's very important to collect everything you couldn't do because of the injury. Save letters, emails, text-messages and other things that describe the reason you cancelled an event.

Will you remember all the things your doctor told you when the insurance company phones you in six months? Hardly. That's why you should note down everything immediately after a doctor's visit and after being in contact with anyone regarding your back pain. Even phone calls. Ask your doctor to get medical certificates that explain your problems.

You may be forced to make a claim if you have been in a car accident.

2. Notify your employer

To get compensation for your sick-leave you have to notify your employer the first day. You can't get compensation retroactively, and in case it takes time, you are losing money. The employer may need to find a substitue for you or change work schedules around. If you don't notify him the first day, this will look very bad. You will also need medical evidence or a fit note from your doctor if you are unable to work for more than 7 days.

3. Contact your insurance company

Phone the insurance company within three days, preferably the first day, and let them know what happened, even if you haven't done anything wrong and don't know the extent of the damage. Many insurance companies can also take a claim online where you can write a damage report and get back to them with more information about the injury once you know it's full extent.

4. Collect physical evidence

This may feel a little "overkill", but it's better to be prepared than to realise that you should've done things differently.

Go to the place of the accident or where your back pain started. What could have caused it? If you can't take things with you: **Take photos.** Also photograph the location, the things involved or that could have been involved and the surroundings. Also take photos of your injuries, such as bruises and so on before you see your doctor. Sometimes it can take time to get an appointment and some marks may have disappeared by then. By taking photos you show that you're meticulous and they can also help to figure out what the real cause is behind the injury. If you can't go to the place where the accident or injury took place, note down the name of the person who prevented you from going there and the time, so that you can go to that person's superior and explain the situation and ask for pictures anyway.

If you can, get witnesses that can support your story or give more details than you may remember – or that could support that people have previously been hurt in that area. You're in a hurry here: People forget easily. Write down names, addresses, phone numbers and all the information they give you. Make sure the person reads through the notes and preferably signs them before you leave. If it's a bigger accident, try to get the witnesses to write down their impressions and sign it themselves.

5. Document your injuries

Visit a doctor as quickly as you can, so that you get an accurate description of your injuries. Make sure visible marks are photographed. A lot of people forget this, which means that they don't have any medical documentation of serious injuries. Save all receipts, bills, letters and other documentation.

Step 2: Determine the matter of blame

In some cases, it's clear who or what carries the blame, but that's far from all cases. Among other things, the question of blame determines how much compensation you'll get from an insurance company.

If you've been in a major accident (like a car crash), this may be something the police takes care of, but more often than not, it's the insurance company, or if the accident took place in the work place, a representative from the Human Resource department that investigates the situation.[72]

The more you can help them, the better. Your notes, photographs and other evidence will serve you well here.

Not all insurance companies want your best but try to avoid giving you any compensation at all. To avoid that situation...

72 Arbetsgivaren anmäler då saken till Arbetsmiljöverket via en blankett på http://www.av.se eller genom att beställa blanketten via telefon.

Do this:

Your main attitude should be helpful, but on your terms.

1. Don't downplay your situation

Before you know the full extent of the injury, it's easy to downplay it. ”Oh, it wasn't that bad.” But if you have that attitude when you're in contact with the insurance company they will believe you and that will lower your chances of getting compensation. Think carefully about the consequences the injury has brought with it. What will this mean for your future? Will it limit things you would've otherwise done?

2. Use the information you've gathered

By collecting information, you've got the ”answers”. Make sure you follow that information when you fill in documents, so that dates and other details are correct. If something is unclear on the form, don't guess. Phone them and ask for a clarification. If you guess and put in the wrong information, the insurance company may not need to compensate you. Be very specific when you contact the insurance company, since you're often sent around without getting help. Prepare your specific question so that it will be harder to send you to another department.

3. Make sure that the dialogues take place through letters

The more of the conversation that is available in paper form, the easier it is for you to do the right thing. It's also harder for them to outsmart you. Get into the habit of sending an email or letter where you note down what was said during the phone call as soon as you finish on the phone. Save copies of all outgoing emails and letters.

4. You don't have to show everything

You may want to please the insurance company when they ask for more information. That's why this might be the most important point! *Too much information isn't always a good thing.*

Let me give you an example: If you allow the insurance company to see your full medical history, you've made it easier for them to point out some minor detail that might have been the cause of your problem. If you don't think that this only happens in awful America and not in Sweden, let me tell you, it happens all the time. Especially people who have had a whiplash injury are affected. Hopefully, we'll see a better protection in this area in the future.[73] Also check out https://www.gov.uk/data-protection for more information.

Your records are really a tool for those who deal with your health. The records are confidential, but you have the right to see what's in it.[74] For example, you'll find information about the diagnosis and treatments you have received in the records.

5. Keep making notes

Write down all the promises, statements and other comments that representatives from the insurance company make. If they promise something positive for you, quickly send a confirmation of that ("As Nils Andersson promised me over a phone conversation..."). Send it in through snail mail/regular mail. Save a copy for yourself. But remember to not be content as soon as they offer the smallest of compensations. Chances are that they're trying to buy you before you realise how much money you could've received.

---

73 Läs till exempel *Dagens medicin*: http://www.dagensmedicin.se/nyheter/2010/03/05/starkare-skydd-for-uppgift/index.xml

74 Läs mer om din journal och vad som gäller på Vårdguidens webbplats: http://www.vardguiden.se/Sa-funkar-det/Lagar--rattigheter/Din-journal/

Step 3: The insurance company

Without a good relationship with the insurance company, you risk going without compensation, which in the long run will increase your stress and therefore also you back pain, so from the perspective of a back expert, I'm telling you: Create a good relationship with them.

A and o in a relationship with the insurance company, lies in understanding how they work. They have all the cards, so you have to follow their rules. You can read most of these rules on their website or in their pamphlets, and since the rules are changed almost monthly, I can't describe them. What I can describe are their basic rules, that you should follow. They are:

1. How you look and act matters. If you dress like a homeless person that has been run over by a bus, you'll be working uphill with the rest of the list. Dress as if you're going to a job interview. In actual fact, that's almost what most of these meetings are about.

2. You have to be active in your rehabilitation, otherwise you'll lose your benefits. If your doctor recommends a treatment or an action, and you forget or aren't bothered to do it, those benefits may be cancelled.

3. There are rules that the employees of insurance companies find unfair, but they don't have a choice in the matter, they still have to be professional.

4. A big reason for why it takes so long to make a decision within is that there's a "decision anguish" taking place. They have to be able to prove to their superiors that there is sufficient paperwork for everything.

In return for following these rules, you should definitely ask for copies for all of their papers, so that you don't misunderstand anything. Make this one of your basic rules: Document everything!

It's their obligation to explain all the papers and decisions, so if you're wondering about something, ask them straight up. They won't tell you anything unless you ask. In many cases, they don't even fully understand the rules themselves... To pretend that they have made a decision to then not follow through on what you agreed on is one cause for why claims are cancelled, so these are important matters.

Step 4: Move on

For most people, these three steps are enough, but if you're in trouble and need to go even further you may need someone who knows laws and the system on your side. You can search on http://solicitors.lawsociety.org.uk or online for phrases that are relevant to your ailment plus solicitor.

EPILOUGE

"The basic difference between an ordinary man and a warrior is that a warrior takes everything as a challenge while an ordinary man takes everything as a blessing or a curse."

– Carlos Castaneda (1925-1988), Brazilian author, in "A seperate reality", 1971

What are you doing tomorrow?

”Last night I made a thousand plans. This morning I went about my business like usual.”

– Konfucius (555 B.C-479 B.C), Chinese philosopher

The book has almost come to an end. This is the book I would’ve wanted when my back pain was at its worst.

I know that most people that have read this book has become pain free by now, since the body has had some time to heal itself. There’s no point in denying that it is the patients’ bodies that do most of my work.

But, if you’ve completed the 12 Inconvenient Back Challenges in this book, then that’s helped your body a lot along the way, too. Besides, you’re 12 boulders lighter now, which must be a relief. And you should also be proud. *I’m* proud of you.

Without those 12 boulders in your backpack, your life should have changed a lot. What new possibilities have you discovered since you stopped complaining for example? How often do you do the 80/20 analysis? How did you do when you swam the English Channel? Please let me know what happened on http://www.ryggexpertarnaljuger.se after you read the book. The best contributions will be rewarded!

If you on the other hand, feel like the book is missing something, take a look at the website. There’s a lot of material that couldn’t be included in the book due to lack of space. If you think of any aspect that I’ve completely missed, then I’ll reward you, too.

Some of the readers will have gotten to this point in the book without having completed the 12 Inconvenient Back Challenges. If you are one of them and are angry and disappointed that your back pain hasn’t improved from this book – either. Then it may be about time you take a long hard look in the mirror. Ask yourself: ”If this was my last day in life, would I be doing what I have planned to do today?” In other words, are you living the life you could be living? Is the answer is ’no’, then maybe you should change that.

Whether you've done all the 12 challenges, or some of them, or none at all, there's still one question that remains unanswered.

What are you doing tomorrow?

BIBLIOGRAPHY

TIPS FOR BOOKS YOU DON'T NEED TO READ

My patients have usually read a few books about back pain before they see me. Some have even read so many that they've moved on from thinking about their back pain to trying to become back experts themselves. Don't make that mistake, too. One or two books are enough, especially if you want to get rid of the pain quickly.

It may go against your gut feeling and I recommend that you don't find out too much, especially considering how long it takes to read one book, you may not get much out of book two, three and so on.

That's why this chapter doesn't include any lists of books. I know that you won't read all of them anyway. But if you're still planning on reading some books, these should be right at the top of your list.

Start here!

Before I wrote *Back Secrets*, I kept recommending these four books again and again. I even bought copies of them and gave them to people I thought might need them and they've always been well-liked by those people. Now I recommend them to you:

The 80/20 Principle

By Richard Koch

This book will teach you how to find focus and prioritise. By doing this, you will decrease your stress.

Healing back pain

By John E. Sarno

Sarno's book teaches you how stress, anger and frustrations could be the cause of your back pain and shows you how to find a path away from this. It's a must for those of you who have suffered from back pain for a long time.

The 7 habits of highly effective people

By Stephen R Covey[75]

Covey's book teaches you what's important in life, and how you put together a plan to make it happen. If you've always wanted a lot of things but haven't made anything happen, then this is the perfect book for you.

Treating your back & neck pain for dummies

By Loic Burn, Michael S Sinel, William W Deardorff

This is a book for those of you who like facts and is a bit of a know-it-all. Read this in-depth book so that you're ready to take on and fight any back expert.

75

THANK YOU

Before I wrote a book, I never used to read these ”Thank you” pages. I know better now. Because these pages tell you how the book came about.

That’s why I’d like to thank Vulkan, led by Linda Skugge and Peter Norrman for such a great service for first time authors. Since Swedish proof reading isn’t my strong suit, I would also like to thank my proof readers.

I’d also like to thank my two friends in armour for these years: Emil Janitzek, you’re priceless, and my lawyer Paul Alwindi for the incredible help.

Robert Capotondi (http://capotondi.se) came with valuable advice about writing blocks, Stefan Engeseth (http://www.detectivemarketing.com/) helped me become more authentic towards myself.

Also, thank you to all the patients and colleagues through the years. You’ve taught me patience as well as how wonderful the world is.

A special thank you to Lennart Guldbrandsson, the person I’ve brain stormed with throughout this entire process. Your wise words, advice and support have been priceless and the result would be nowhere near as good without you, my friend.

Finally, I’d like to thank my parents that loved me even when I didn’t deserve it. The love, stability, knowledge and life joy you have given me and my brother has been an incredible foundation to stand on.

INDEX

1. The 12 inconvenient back challenges

2. Search words

NSAID
Pain killers
Patient
Placebo
The parts of the back
–
The spine
Tilt table
Sex
Physiotherapist
Shoes
Sleep
Strength training
Williamson, Marianne
Yoga

3.

Robin Wakeham has a master's degree in orthopaedic manual therapy and has worked as a physiotherapist since 2001 in Sweden, Great Britain and in the US. His e-commerce sites with products for people with back pain have pulled in many thousands of pounds, but he became much more content in life when he started to focus on his family instead. He also has many years of experience as a back patient since an ice-hockey accident in 1984, a fall from a scaffolding in 1996, and extreme weight loss in 2006 when his bum would no longer support his too long tailbone. Nowadays, he's running a successful back pain clinic in Stockholm.

Made in the USA
Thornton, CO
05/18/23 02:35:30

613cdf56-df94-4baa-9139-05f4280a9578R02